REAL WOMEN INVEST in REAL ESTATE

THE WISE WOMAN'S GUIDE TO REAL ESTATE
INVESTING AND ACHIEVING FINANCIAL SECURITY

UDO MARYANNE OKONJO

authorHOUSE®

AuthorHouse™ UK
1663 Liberty Drive
Bloomington, IN 47403 USA
www.authorhouse.co.uk
Phone: 0800 047 8203 (Domestic TFN)
         +44 1908 723714 (International)

© 2018 Udo Maryanne Okonjo. All rights reserved.

No part of this book may be reproduced, stored in a retrieval system, or transmitted by any means without the written permission of the author.

Published by AuthorHouse 06/28/2019

ISBN: 978-1-5462-9005-6 (sc)
ISBN: 978-1-5462-9009-4 (e)

Print information available on the last page.

Any people depicted in stock imagery provided by Getty Images are models, and such images are being used for illustrative purposes only.
Certain stock imagery © Getty Images.

This book is printed on acid-free paper.

Because of the dynamic nature of the Internet, any web addresses or links contained in this book may have changed since publication and may no longer be valid. The views expressed in this work are solely those of the author and do not necessarily reflect the views of the publisher, and the publisher hereby disclaims any responsibility for them.

DEDICATION

This book is dedicated to my daughters, Chidi and Anwuli, such amazing young ladies who make me so proud and who inspire me daily by their strength and wisdom. To my mum, Josephine Ada Kachikwu, I don't thank you enough. But you showed me the way to be a Real Woman. To every 'Finer Woman', of the Finer Wealth Investment Club who understand that they too can build a solid purposeful and inspiring future and need no permission to do so. We created the Finer Wealth Club whose core vision is to give women and by extension their families access to insight and opportunities to aid Intelligent Real Estate Investments. Finally, to my dear husband and all men who support and encourage their wives, daughters, sisters, and girl friends to be financially empowered. You are wise men. I salute you all.

ACKNOWLEDGEMENTS

I have no idea how this book would have been possible without the prodding and help of the champions at Fine and Country who basically make my work so much easier. I'm grateful to work with such excellent men and women. This book is a testament to your true championship DNA.

CONTENTS

Introduction: Why Real Estate Rocks xix
The Backdrop: Keeping It Real xxiii

A: Assessment and Appreciation 1
B: Belief 8
C: Cash Flow, Contracts, Commissions, Control, and Community 13
D: Due Diligence and Discounted or Distressed Properties 18
E: Equity 22
F: Finance and Financial Discipline 24
G: Goals and Guidelines 31
H: Hold 36
I: Insurance 38
J: Joint Venture 41
K: Knowledge and Keeping Track 46
L: Land 49
M: Mortgages and Management 54
N: Negotiation 59
O: Observe Growth Patterns 61
P: Prime Location 63
Q: Questions 67
R: Referrals and Reputation 70
S: Solutions and Strategies 72
T: Title and Terms 75
U: Understanding 77
V: Valuation and Value 79

W: Waiting 86
X: X-Ray Lens 88
Y: You 89
Z: Z? 91

FOREWORD

Anything that gives a woman a measure of financial independence and confidence is immensely valuable. One must congratulate Udo Okonjo for the exemplary zeal she has shown in supporting the growth and development of women across a wide range of activities and disciplines and thank her for sharing in *'Real Women Invest in Real Estate'* the impressive range of knowledge she has gained during her own journey through this fascinating world.

In writing this book Udo has continued her impressive tradition of adding to the store of knowledge, wisdom and skill that benefits all women - and indeed anyone who reads this book. In her usual engaging and informative manner Udo has shared important considerations to bear in mind when thinking of a real estate investment as well as tips and tricks that are both achievable and practical. The anecdotes and real life examples she discusses help any reader to better assess their own circumstances thereby enhancing their ability to avoid the occasional pitfalls that can potentially affect any investment and, in so doing, becoming much more competent and confident investors. We look forward to much more from this author.

Dr. Myma A. Belo-Osagie
Founding Partner
Udo Udoma & Belo-Osagie

PRAISES FOR *REAL WOMEN INVEST IN REAL ESTATE*

Real Women Invest in Real Estate is an amazing book! Brilliant Udo Okonjo who has walked the talk, bridges gaps of knowledge and practicality in real estate investment, simplifies, gives clarity, inspires women to invest in real estate in such a way that you gain confidence to do so, fears are erased when you have the practical tools and this is what this book will do for any woman or anyone who reads it. The practical stories of other women will build your confidence and assure you that you too can do it. No more delaying in investing at any level of real estate.

The best time to start is now, secure your future and your unborn generations. When women are empowered this way, it saves families, women have the capacity to be excellent managers of wealth, this book will unleash that potential in you.

*She considered a field and buys it, says the good book!

*Let's step up to eradicate poverty one woman at a time.

—**Nike Adeyemi**, founder, Real Woman Foundation
  International Speaker, social reformer, life coach, author

When I think Real Estate, I think Udo Okonjo. Few experts make this outstanding asset class as exciting, inviting and attainable.

Whilst Nigerian women have made huge strides in business, in the corporate world and in government, and continue to strengthen their earning power and influence, far too many women still feel ill equipped to make bold financial decisions.

A lack of knowledge is just one of the reasons why many women remain on the sidelines; but even more glaring is the issue of confidence. Women tend to be afraid of making bad investment decisions, losing money and just not knowing how to get started.

"Real Women invest in Real Estate," adopts a conversational, engaging style as well as real life stories that illustrate the power of real estate. Thanks to Udo, readers will certainly gain "clarity, confidence, and competence" in their journey up the property ladder.

—Nimi Akinkugbe
    CEO Bestman Games
    Founder "Money Matters with Nimi"

In this book, Udo Okonjo has touched on the major factors that make real estate investment an essential move for everyone. The need for better financial returns and the focus on buying something tangible, that supports other financial decisions in the future cannot be underestimated. The status and maturity of mind you attain by being a property owner and investor watching your portfolio grow fills you with pride especially, for women who have lost their mothers. You can almost feel their respect, after years of complaining of your frivolity on holidays.

Udo Okonjo has certainly provided needful insight and clarity in an asset class that can appear daunting.

—Betty Kachikwu
    CEO SIGNATURE SUITES LTD

In line with her passion to empower women, generous Udo Okonjo shares priceless nuggets which light the way to sound real estate investment for all: from beginners to those in the C Suite.

Aside from clearly identifying steps which need to be taken prior to and during the process of investing; Udo Okonjo highlights intangible holistic considerations every investor should seriously think about. Real estate is not only about bricks and mortar; it is an enabling tool; a lifestyle; an inheritance.

Udo Okonjo leaves her readers clear about how to power a purpose-driven life with real estate.

—Catherine Bickersteth
Nurturing world-class intellect

A riveting page turner with great insights and sound advice evidently born from a wealth and depth of experience.

This book as seen through the lense of Udo Okonjo, a 21st century female change maker and thought leader, provides practical & structured modern day advice on wealth creation through sustainable property investment. **A must read, not limited to women.**

—Dr. Nneka Abulokwe, UK
My real estate adventure.

I had always been interested in real estate - just not the way it was done in Lagos in the mid-2000s. That was until Udo and her team presented me with an off- plan opportunity in South Africa that promised me investment protection in a safe environment. Thus began my real estate adventure and I have since bought a couple in Nigeria- especially via the off-plan option. My advice to every woman who has some disposable income-just start! Find a development that meets your budget, do your research and dive right in. The shoes, bags, jewellery and clothes will soon be forgotten. Sound property investment provides you appreciable income and security no matter the season.

Great insight and definitely a worthwhile guide for both the aspiring and astute investor.

—Uzo Nwani

Like many of Udo's fans, I often wonder where she gets the continual positive energy and verve for life and work. She is constantly sharing her knowledge to motivate, uplift and empower women. Funnily enough, I have done likewise in my 26 years of running a real estate business; 80% of my clients have been women.

The title of Udo's book is sophisticated, a guide to "investing" however, from my experience I would have used "acquisition". Women acquire property. I suspect that the "investment" part is a benefit rather than their goal.

People are always asking me, "How come most of your clients are women, not men?" I think it is because, women are truly the "wise" ones when they find real estate that they can afford. Most men would certainly not buy from a developer when they believe they could build it cheaper, faster, better and actually larger; even though what they have in their pocket is a fraction of the cost or they wait till they have accumulated enough money then they build their dream house. You hardly hear of a woman building a dream house!

All the women I have worked with would not consider building a dream house until they had finished all the most important things in their lives such as helping to educate their children, keeping the house together, supporting their partner in his decisions, or building their business/growing their career. All these must come first before the dream project, unlike their male counterparts.

One of the amazing traits of women is they are super realistic. I want a house to live in because I don't want to pay rent anymore. Now, how do I acquire a place and not pay rent? I want two houses, or a house and a flat. One to live in, one to rent out for my children's school fees and later for my child to live in.

I have to be realistic and honest about what my pocket can afford. After deducting the cost of living, school fees etc. I will put the rest into property.

Most women are patient; they have other income, a job, business, or income from a partner before acquiring. They look for small affordable units, always in areas they can live in. You are unlikely to find many women buying an office building in the business district when she can buy a row of residential homes. The closest to commercial that they prefer is retail spaces.

In making their real estate decisions, women use simple principles like social connections, referrals, friends who have bought this, or from the same place and developer, people they know whose concepts appeal to their taste, the reputation of the developer. This is quite interesting because sophisticated male investors use these same criteria for business investment principles that have made them huge returns in the world of business not only using ROI or ROE. However, when men are making real estate decisions, they allow their egos to take the lead with often disastrous results.

Most of my female clients when acquiring real estate, never tell anyone not even friends, family. In some cases they don't even tell their spouses until the deal is concluded. Contrast that with most men in business who let people know they are "involved" in a deal.

What I like about Udo's book is that while it may appear like the fundamentals for those women who have already acquired property, it will give confidence to those who are scared of spending such large amounts of money in case it goes wrong; the risk averse woman.

It will serve as a go to book for women who do not have people to ask, or feel that they don't have people they can trust. Women who do not want their nearest and dearest to know that they have accumulated enough money to make a real estate acquisition or investment

The real estate industry needs more women to participate. They are an underutilized economic force. They are great savers and safe borrowers. They have capital earning less than 10% return in financial institutions when they could be earning between 15% and 45% in real estate as well as see the value of their real estate appreciate to such an extent that it can cushion them from the shocks of a reversal of fortune, a divorce or loss of a dependable source of income.

I have seen this happen many times; when that small affordable house is sold for 5 to 10 times the acquisition price and then 2 years later, after recovering, the woman replaces it with another acquisition.

I look forward to seeing a surge in female participation in real estate for the benefit of the entire economy to give women more financial independence, and establish a status of greater respect for women in their homes and our society.

—Gbolly Balogun
CEO
County Estate Limited
Real Estate Developers and Consultants.

INTRODUCTION

WHY REAL ESTATE ROCKS

'[S]he is not a full [wo]man who does not own a piece of land.' – Hebrew proverb

I became interested in real estate; in my early thirties. I was practicing as a corporate and commercial lawyer while running a boutique pot-and-art gallery called Zanzibar—a passion project. I recall stumbling across a reproduced copy of *Nothing Down* by Robert Allen, who became my long-distance real estate mentor before I met him in person many years later in Johannesburg. His two books, *Creating Wealth* and *Nothing Down,* became bibles for my early forays into real estate investment. By practicing some of the power principles in his books and seeing the results, I got hooked on real estate as a sound pathway to financial security.

Most important, real estate investment gave me wings to fly. Investing in real estate gave me the freedom I needed to make decisions that aligned with my passion and values. I really liked practicing law but needed the versatility of generating additional income and growing my finances without slaving over hundreds of pages of contracts. In addition, the flexibility became a saving grace when I later encountered a life-threatening breast cancer scare. I loved being able to invest in any location, applying the same real estate principles. I've recently heard stories of many amazing women who testified that their real estate investments gave them the arsenal they needed to overcome health and other life challenges. One woman had walked away from a high-profile, well-paid job to pursue her passion without the constraints of workplace harassment. During these past years, I've been able to figure out what truly matters in life. I realise that with financial freedom comes an ability to be more, do more, and give more. If approached correctly, real estate truly rocks. It allows you to live fully and work on your own terms. At least it did for me.

I have always believed that there are no extraordinary people, only ordinary people who applied extraordinary principles consistently to achieve mastery. In the same way, there are no extraordinary investors or investments, only extraordinary principles applied by ordinary people to achieve extraordinary investments. I have learnt by experience and through research that anyone can profit from real estate, if you play by the rules.

I'm a firm believer in principles because I have seen their impact on my own life, business, and investments. It is common knowledge that the simpler the principles are, the easier they are to apply. That's why I often use alphabetical frameworks to convey numerous messages during speaking engagements and in writings. Using the alphabet to explain concepts is a fun, simple, but engaging way that everyone can relate to.

This book is meant to be an introductory guide to successful principles for anyone to climb on the property ladder, with style, ease, and expertise. I hope it will help you set and achieve your financial goals using real estate as a building block.

Recently, while trying to decide how to express my unwavering passion to live an impactful life, which includes empowering women (and men who honour and respect them), Bob Allen encouraged me to combine all the elements of my passions: purposeful living and wealth creation through real estate and entrepreneurship. This guide is therefore part of my attempt to help more people create wealth, so that they can live more purposeful and successful lives and, hopefully, impact others. Consider this book a practical guide to enable you to invest more confidently and achieve financial security so that you have the power to decide in favour of yourself and express your life's gifting, impacting the world without the pressure of financial constraints.

I encourage you to follow the example of a dear friend of mine, a woman who I believe is a fitting role model, with her ability to multitask and invest wisely and live an incredibly impactful life. I believe her real estate investment played a significant role in her ability to do so much, including investing in her business and contributing to her family and society, just like the woman in Proverbs 31:16:

'She considers a field and buys it: From her earnings she plants a vineyard'

Udo Okonjo
The Cunningham

THE BACKDROP

KEEPING IT REAL

'Now, one thing I tell everyone is learn about real estate. Repeat after me: real estate provides the highest returns, the greatest values, and the least risk.' – Armstrong Williams

The Nigerian real estate sector has recorded consistent growth over the last four years. The market is valued at ₦6.5 trillion and estimated to grow at an average of 10 per cent annually for several years. The following facts are also interesting to note:

- The sector contributed 7.57 per cent to Nigeria's GDP in 2015.
- The country requires 17 to 20 million housing units to address the housing deficit.
- Nigeria attracted $3.96 billion (about ₦780.12 billion) in real estate development in 2014, which represents 11 per cent of the total sum of $36.4 billion expended on infrastructure construction projects in the country.
- Eighty per cent of the adult population in Nigeria live in rented apartments, compared to 20 per cent in Ghana and 25 per cent in South Africa.

- Nigeria has a low homeownership rate of less than 25 per cent, lower than that of Indonesia (84 per cent), Kenya (73 per cent), and South Africa (56 per cent). The major issues that continue to affect housing in Nigeria include inadequate access to financing, slow administrative procedures, and the high cost of land registration and titling. These data represent real opportunities. Real estate has been identified as a major contributor to the Nigerian economy, although traditionally viewed as a man's domain and playing field. However, as the concept of a woman's place being only in the kitchen is replaced by women playing leading roles in both boardrooms and in their own businesses, we are witnessing first-hand the growing trend of women climbing onto the real estate ladder and staying there firmly.

More women are actively investing in real estate as an asset class. At my company, Fine and Country West Africa, a good percentage of our clients are female entrepreneurs and professionals. About 30 per cent of our clients in the residential investment category at the mid-premium price range are female entrepreneurs, professionals, and executives.

We also have a good number of young female investors. When I started real estate fifteen years ago, first as an investor and then subsequently as an adviser, broker, and real estate entrepreneur, women were my core constituency. I remember approaching a few professional women in the banking sector and working with them to put together some money. I would say to these women, 'Instead of buying that bag, a thousand here and there could go a long way towards a down payment on a property.'

For some of those early property investments, the reservation deposit required was approximately $2,000 (the equivalent then of about ₦300,000).

Over the years, I have had a natural affinity for working with women, and it's been interesting to see that women invest in a unique way. Women who invest often have a certain tentativeness and lack of confidence. I strongly believe that this is mainly a result of societal conditioning and, in some cases, arises from a lack of knowledge. Some women may not be aware of the impact that investing in property can have on future financial well-being and the ability to make better decisions.

If we've come this far by investing tentatively, imagine what could happen if we were armed with the right information to boost our confidence. Then we could really begin to take advantage of the investment opportunities that abound.

I'm particularly proud that some of our female clients and friends, as they've grown more confident, are making significant investments, and so much good has come out of it. A friend once shared with me how she got through a great health challenge. It was her real estate portfolio that gave her the freedom to leave her work and go to a distant part of the world to get treated successfully. Financial freedom and the ability to make better decisions are two of the benefits of investing in real estate.

Staying in Real Control of Your Finances and Destiny

Real estate investing is no longer exclusively a man's world. More women are getting involved in real estate as a viable way of generating income and building wealth. Some women are flipping houses (buying properties and reselling them) and making profits on their capital within a short time, while other women approach real estate investment from a long-term perspective. Their strategy is to buy properties, fix them up, and then hold onto them for the long term, renting to a growing population of tenants. Others collaborate to invest in larger commercial projects. Many, however, remain stuck and unable to climb onto the real estate ladder due to a lack of confidence and know-how.

For International Women's Day 2016, I wrote an article, 'Beyond Parity', for *BusinessDay,* Nigeria's leading financial and business publication. I wrote that women need to climb the real estate ladder and achieve some measure of financial freedom. When I say 'financial freedom', I'm referring to the ability to make decisions in your favour, whether in the corporate world or at home, because women are vulnerable at many levels, even at the highest levels in families.

The benefits of women investing are numerous. You are able to walk away from a role that doesn't serve you, or you can make decisions even while in that role because you know that you have options. I believe that financial security makes you a more purposeful person, able to operate more effectively because you have choices and are not driven by desperation or fear.

This played out recently when a good friend of mine told me that she had left a well-paying, high-profile job because of certain corporate issues that didn't go with her personal value system. She said to me, even before I asked for any details, 'Udo, do you know it's my real estate investments [that gave me the freedom to do this]? I started investing in real estate at age twenty-five.'

And I thought, *Wow!*

I share several stories in this book; it's not an overly formal read. This isn't a book about the corporate side to investing in real estate. It's about destinies and nation-building; everyone knows women are nation-builders, architects of society. Even as partners at home, it is increasingly important that women take their rightful positions as well-equipped and savvy investors when making decisions with their spouses. The era of sitting pretty served no useful purpose and left women in a vulnerable position.

I also share stories from some amazing women, including Mrs Ibukun Awosika, Ms Angela Aneke, Mrs Subu Giwa-Amu, and Mrs Bola Adesola, CEO of Standard Chartered Bank.

Ibukun Awosika is the chairwoman of the board of directors of First Bank Nigeria Limited. She also sits on several other boards, including House of Tara (which she chairs), Digital Jewel PLC, and Cadbury Nigeria Limited. She is the founder and chief executive officer of the Chair Centre Group. 'A lot of women are intimidated by the issue of building wealth,' she noted at a FINER Wealth Series, organised jointly by our company, Fine and Country, and First Bank Private Banking. Culturally, she noted, women are brought up to think somebody else is responsible for building the wealth on their behalf, and they are meant to benefit from it.

I agree with Mrs Awosika. It is my intention to correct this mindset, and other faulty ones, by sharing simple but empowering principles and stories from women who have climbed onto the real estate ladder and remain firmly on it.

Angela Aneke is a successful real estate investor and a former executive director at United Bank for Africa. For her, it's important not to see yourself first as a woman but, rather, as a competent professional, entrepreneur, or whatever else you do. Yes, you are a woman, she said, but you don't have to go into business with a mindset that holds you back or makes you feel less competent. You are a human being. You are a professional. 'Don't think men are more confident,' she said. 'In fact, don't even have in your mind, "I'm a woman." I sat on a board committee where I was the only woman.'

Subu Giwa-Amu, a seasoned banker with over twenty-seven years' experience in commercial banking, is the CEO of Brookstone Investment and Properties Limited, a real estate/financial consultancy firm. She is also the CEO of Textures and Colours. She's invested successfully in both residential and commercial real estate and feels passionate about using it as a route to securing a solid financial and purposeful future.

Over the years, these women and many of our female clients have inspired others about wealth creation through investing in real estate, starting small, seeing the results, and gaining confidence as a result of taking action.

What's Your Excuse?

If you're thinking real estate is only for the rich, think again.

An entrepreneur once told me that many years ago, she gave an employee ₦20,000. The young woman bought a plot of land in Badagry, Lagos, which appreciated over the years. A day came when the land had to be taken over due to ongoing road work, and this young woman received a compensation of ₦3 million. Imagine the power that three million naira (approximately $10,000 at the time of writing) gave that young woman, who very likely hadn't been earning much. Women at all levels can enjoy the benefits of real estate.

Mrs Bola Adesola, CEO of Standard Chartered Bank and an ardent believer in the power of real estate investing as a strong pathway to financial independence, said that she constantly encourages young female professionals to start investing early; she jokes that she even bullies them into giving up the frivolous spending that tends to keep them stuck in consumer mode, with no real assets. She raised the importance of women investing in real estate and noted specifically that women tend to outlive men and carry a huge burden of aged parents and children, which tends to hinder their abilities to invest. She shared this while speaking at a Women and Wealth Breakfast held in Lagos in early 2017. The truth is that women tend to put themselves last and even jeopardise their long-term welfare for others. Committing to investing in a long-term asset class that is not very liquid could help them become more financially disciplined because it's usually the cash at hand without a purpose that tends to be at risk.

The Stiletto Edge

When I look at our society and how degraded our environment is, from Benin to Lagos, Sokoto to Abuja, I remember that research has shown that your environment actually affects your quality of life. I believe that women can bring something to the conversations about our skylines, about building the future of a society where we all enjoy well-being. Women are uniquely configured to add value to real estate as a result of our nurturing vision and the quest to solve societal problems. Housing units for millennials, old people, and vulnerable people are all real estate opportunities, providing social infrastructure that benefits society and provides financial rewards; women can bring a unique perspective to these areas and indeed across all aspects of the real estate market.

It is my desire for more women to get on the property ladder, climb it with style and common sense, and stay firmly on it.

In this book, I will be sharing stories, concepts, principles, and strategies that will guide you on how you can get started (or gain more ground if you've already started).

There is more territory for us to take. There are new communities to build, more functional offices to serve small entrepreneurs and big companies alike; there's just so much we can do in the real estate space, either as investors or along the value chain where you can put your foot onto the real estate ladder and related services, from production/construction to distribution, facility management, interior design, and even architecture. This book, however, covers mainly residential real estate, as it is the safest and easiest aspect of real estate for a first-timer or early-stage investor to deal with. The principles I share, however, are universally applicable.

This book is born out of my desire to empower women to make better financial choices; it's based on personal experiences and corporate engagements with clients in the course of my legal and real estate journey. Real estate investing has been one of the most powerful things that I've experienced in my adult life. I was a practicing corporate lawyer, and when I got in contact with real estate, it almost literally saved my life, just like the lady who shared about her health challenges and how real estate contributed to her being able to take care of herself.

In my case, it gave me the freedom to stop everything, relocate for a while, refocus, and press the restart button; in fact, I acquired the Fine and Country licence while I was recovering from early-stage breast cancer in 2006. I was able to focus on giving myself some much-needed tender loving care, be there for my children, read and write, and reflect on life, without the pressure of working at the same pace as I did before my diagnosis. After my treatment, I deliberately chose to retain that lifestyle of purposefully undertaking only meaningful, enjoyable work, with clients I trust, like, and respect. My investments in real estate made this largely possible, giving me the ability to choose in my favour.

DETERRENT TO ABUSE

A case can also be made for financial independence as a deterrent to abuse in relationships. There is convincing evidence that physical and emotional violence against lower income women, including the working class, has escalated as the income disparity between men and women widens. Many professional women remain in abusive marital and professional relationships because of low incomes and a lack of financial independence (in some cases, fear of not having a roof over their heads). Sometimes, they suffer abuse both at home and in the workplace.

International Women's Day 2017 was celebrated with the theme 'Be Bold for Change.' In the first year after a divorce, a woman's standard of living drops an average of 73 per cent; women are staying single longer and live much longer than men on the average, even when married. Within their lifetime, more than 80 per cent of all women will invariably be solely responsible for their financial well-being and need to take charge of their investments. In addition, women in Nigeria contribute actively to their families' expenses, in most cases sacrificing everything for school fees, living costs, and family expenses, leaving them unprepared for their retirement years. How can we encourage more women to take control of their financial independence through getting on the real estate ladder after taking care of the basic expenses and savings? With investment in real estate at any level, women can become more confident, whether in the workplace or at home.

Some of the challenges that arise with regards to attaining parity between both genders in real estate investments include local traditions which stifle a woman's sense of confidence in investing in real estate, the fear of appearing to be too masculine, and seeming too independent. Many women invest in secret, thereby losing confidence or running the risk of not going through the proper due process with unprofessional agents (who may even take advantage of this secrecy). I've had cases where women were worried about letting their spouses and their families know they were investing because of the fear of being labelled overly ambitious. I know a lot of professional women who still feel that real estate investment should be left to men.

There are no legal barriers to real estate for women any more. Thankfully, the Supreme Court recently overruled the laws in Igboland that prevented women from inheriting land. Other barriers are being shattered at many levels and in various parts of the country, freeing women to participate in the real estate economy. The Nigerian Land Use Act is universally applicable irrespective of gender, so as women, we have no excuse if we don't invest. Section 43 guarantees every single person the right to acquire immeasurable territory.

Some questions such as inheritance and tax planning still arise, with many women having no access to sophisticated advice on how to structure their investments, especially in a society where women owning significant investments is still frowned upon.

In view of this, it is absolutely vital to place in the hands of women information that will propel them to wealth creation and guide them through the process of investing safely.

As earlier mentioned, women tend to bring a unique eye to real estate; they tend to be more conservative when investing. Even in design, women tend to have an advantage over men and will therefore more than likely position their properties better when selling or renting.

There are no extraordinary investments, only extraordinary principles applied by ordinary people to ordinary projects. Principles are fundamental to success, and the thing to note about principles is that they only work if you work them. Ultimately, though, it is important to see that most of these principles are universally applicable; everyone (men and women) can profit from real estate if they play by the rules. As women, however, we have a stronger incentive to ensure we make these investments work, whether single, married, divorced, or widowed. Irrespective of marital status, women should actively seek to engage in real estate, for themselves and from the point of view of adding value to their personal or family portfolio.

This book contains twenty-six power principles and practical advice that will help you climb the real estate ladder with confidence, style, and expertise. The aim ultimately is for you to become a more important contributor to society as you achieve financial security and make better personal choices. My passion is to educate, encourage, and equip women to build successful lives on their own terms and not be limited by fear and societal constraints. Women are a treasure trove of unlimited possibilities; their creativity can be harnessed to create wealth using real estate as a very significant vehicle.

I know you will succeed when you decide to embrace your dreams of a secure financial future. I did, and I've never looked back.

Finally, remember this: 'It's never too late to start getting wealthy.' – Richard Templar

A

ASSESSMENT AND APPRECIATION

Lack of clarity, purpose, or vision is the biggest risk to a real estate investment, as it is in life, business, or society.

A is therefore for Assessment.

Proverbs 29:18 says, 'Where there is no vision, the people perish, but he that keeps a clear picture of His destination, happy is he.' It is a valuable investment principle.

To profit in real estate, the biggest factor is not just the 'Where' in terms of location, location, location but the 'Why' and 'When.' Lack of clarity, purpose, or vision is the biggest risk to a real estate investment as it is in life, business, or society.

Real estate investing mistakes can be both costly and complicated on many levels. With one fatal error in judgement, an investor could be set back financially and psychologically, essentially perishing on many accounts. It is therefore important to have clarity from the onset about a number of important things.

My role model, the Proverbs 31 woman mentioned earlier, always started her investment by 'considering' a field or a piece of real estate. It costs nothing to consider an opportunity when it presents itself. The best way to get started in investing in any asset class of real estate is by conducting an honest assessment. Take an assessment of your current financial position. No one builds without first counting the cost. Start with a clear vision and goal. Why do you want to invest? What exactly do you want to achieve by investing in real estate? Is your goal long term or short term? Do you want capital growth or cash flow through rental income? There's no reason to not go for both, although the earlier you start, the better your returns over time.

'Don't build wealth for building's sake,' Mrs. Ibukun Awosika said. 'Because there's a point where it becomes a liability. You must know why and to what end.'

The most successful investors have a powerful vision that drives their investment decisions. You must know your 'why.' 'Securing your financial future' may sound vague, but having a property that you intend to use as a collateral for your business in future may be a stronger reason; so is funding your children's education using a particular piece of real estate or building a block of rental apartments to use for your retirement income. Having a solid asset such as real estate, so that you can retire without relying on your children, pursue a long-held lifestyle, or pursue your hobbies without the pressure of structured work can be strong motivating factors to take the plunge into investing. Some may have the motivation of providing clean, safe, and affordable rental housing for the lower to middle class as a pathway to creating wealth while solving a big problem of insufficient housing, thereby impacting society positively.

As a businessperson, owning property serves you when you need collateral for a loan. You can also invest in real estate for pleasure, like a country home in a city that you get away to for a much-needed retreat and rejuvenation, while making it available for others for rent.

In addition to having a clear vision, it is important to know your starting point. If you do not know where you are, it is much more difficult to get direction to a desired destination. Real estate is preferably and most suitable as a long-term play. It takes time to extract liquidity from it, so this is an important consideration when checking what you can afford to invest. A mid-level professional asked me recently what type of property she could invest her savings in (about ₦20 million). I asked if she had set aside savings for her core short-term expenses such as housing, health, and travel, and when I found out she had not, I told her she didn't have ₦20 million to invest. And truth is, she could still make an investment with less than that amount. It's more a question of knowing what you can and cannot invest.

Doing a 360 assessment of your current finances and wealth profile will help you determine how much you can invest. It is important to be true to yourself, as this helps you recognise your real situation and adopt the correct strategy. Are you single, married, monogamous, or in a polygamous relationship (remember we have various shades of polygamy, especially in Africa)? As a married woman, you must know your own husband, know your own circumstance, and know how best to work your circumstance in order to achieve your goals.

Is this a personal, family, or business investment? Is it long term or short term? You need to know because you can't match short-term money with long-term objectives. Is it for cash flow or capital gains? Is it to be used to hedge against inflation, as a store of value, for retirement, or for school fees? Or is it to invest in something major in future? Your starting point and your destination are two critical elements when choosing to invest.

Some time ago, I met an astute investor in Cancun, Mexico, and discussed why he wanted to invest in Oakwood Place, a residential project in Ikoyi sold by Fine and Country West Africa; his absolute clarity struck a chord with me. He said, 'I would like to buy it as a long-term investment and rent it out for rental income, over the next ten years, until I return to Nigeria. It's therefore a rental investment with a future potential owner occupier use in such a great location.'

It seems basic, but having this sort of clarity makes your decisions easier and faster. A good case of the Where, Why, and When converging to make a great investment.

As a lawyer and wealth advisor, I've found many women unfortunately clueless about some of the basic dynamics of their personal finances. In addition, women tend to be naive and may be embarrassed to address their real financial situation. It's important as a woman to become more financially savvy, ask questions about your family finances, take stock of the real estate portfolio of your family, and understand which ones you have access to and what their current status is.

EXERCISE

Take stock of your current real estate holdings. Do you have any? Is it jointly owned? Do you own your own home? Do you have any plots of land or rental property? Have you inherited (or do you stand to inherit) any property from your parents or others?

Do you have any cash savings? Is it in your local or foreign currency? Is it in a savings, a fixed deposit, or a current account? Do you have any stocks? What's the value? Do you know your current net worth? Do you have an accurate, up-to-date indication of your family's assets across all asset classes?

Do you own a small business? Do you rent? Are you in a position to buy and let it out to another small business?

TIP

Do you have any designer bags, jewellery, or similar items that you can dispose of to get started with a personal real estate investment?

For example, eBay is a good starting point because it is anonymous, as far as your immediate circle is concerned (assuming you care). Other online and local platforms handle the sale of designer items. You would be surprised how much you can raise for a down payment for a plot of land. This sense of accomplishment is more powerful than carrying a designer bag with an unclear financial future. If you are a young woman and feel your income is not enough to start investing, consider buying an inexpensive (or cutting out completely) *aso-ebi* for weddings and parties; instead, ask for the colour code and adapt what you have. Just make sure to look great and keep a beautiful smile on your face throughout the party, while you remind yourself of your secret destination.

Never forget that people hardly get richer for owning designer items or spotting the best aso-ebi, but it has been proven that 90 per cent of all millionaires own a significant portfolio of real estate.

Mrs. Awosika summed up this issue of assessment succinctly: 'The most important thing for you is this: decide where you are, decide what you want, check what your own income is, make your plan, and don't listen to anybody that tries to dissuade you.'

A is also for Appreciation. Your investment will generally appreciate over time, especially in a developing economy. Capital appreciation is one of the biggest advantages of real estate investments but should not be the sole target if you want to be a balanced investor. Time works well for real estate; you will always see growth given enough time. You can use this to your advantage by buying whatever is affordable, then when it appreciates, sell what you have and use the proceeds to invest in new, lower priced opportunities. You can also borrow from friends and family or partner with people to buy land and share profit when it appreciates.

Five years ago, Lekki 2 in Lagos was going for ₦5 million per plot. Now, it's selling for about ₦30 million. Waterfront plots in Victoria Garden City, Lagos, now sell for ₦80 and ₦120 million each, when eighteen years ago, those plots sold for ₦5 million. I know a lady who bought four plots of land in Banana Island twenty-five years ago, at ₦7 million each. Today, a plot of land in Banana Island goes for ₦300 to ₦400 million each. She's now a billionaire. At the time, her colleagues may have thought she was too aggressive or not fashion forward enough, because she was buying land when they were buying big bags and designer stilettos.

Appreciation potential is a key consideration in real estate investment. The price of property appreciates based on factors such as infrastructure development, growth of the local economy, availability of land, and transport accessibility/connectivity. If there is a boom in the local economy and commercial development goes up, demand for both residential and commercial properties will reflect the trend.

Another friend shared her own experience investing in real estate. She is living proof that investing in real estate as a woman is possible. She had some foreign currency savings she had accumulated for her children over time, which came to twenty thousand British pounds. She wondered what she could do with it, and a friend who was active in real estate in England suggested she invest in property in Doncaster that cost about ninety thousand pounds. Twenty thousand pounds was accepted as a good down payment. She took an interest-only mortgage and then rented out the property. She was getting monthly rent of 450 pounds, but her mortgage was only 150 pounds every month. So she had extra income monthly. A few years later, she decided she wanted to sell the property because she needed cash to help with school fees. She thought she would get less for it, but she found that the property had appreciated to 160,000 pounds from 90,000, and bear in mind she hadn't paid fully for the property, but she benefitted fully and solely from the appreciation. She promptly changed her mind about selling it and instead extracted equity from the property. We will learn about equity later.

Back when she was about twenty-two years old, she had gone with a group of friends and bought some plots of land in Ajah, but she lost that investment due to *omo nile* guys who swindled them. She could have let this derail her from ever investing in real estate again, but she didn't. Fear of failing serves no useful purpose. All it does is rob you twice over. It's far better to have tried and failed and learnt from your mistakes than to live a life of regret and lack. You'll read more on this in the next principle, 'Belief.'

This same friend has also shared another story that I love so much, 'From Oshodi to Parkview.' She had been looking at setting up a food business close to the airport, having noticed that there weren't good places to eat there at the time. She didn't want to rent the property she would use, so she found a building to buy. It cost ₦13 million, and though she didn't have the money, she borrowed it. She had a dream and believed it was achievable. The food business eventually went down after a couple of years, due to her constant traveling, which led to money being siphoned by staff, but she still had her property standing. A mortgage bank came to her, saying they wanted to use the property for five years, so she leased it to them for ₦25 million.

Before the five years elapsed, she got very sick. She actually had a stroke and experienced several major shifts in her life. At that time, she was living in a rented apartment and needed to own the roof over her head so that if anything happened to her, her children would not be homeless. When the lease period ended, she got several offers, and she eventually sold her property for enough to pay 80 per cent down payment for the five-bedroom house in which she now lives at highbrow Parkview Estate, Ikoyi.

You can get your foot on a rung of the ladder and even start investing in real estate before you own your home. Get started, and experience the power of appreciation.

B

BELIEF

'Failure is part of the process of success. People who avoid failure also avoid success.' – Robert Kiyosaki

B is for belief. Belief is the starting point of all successful endeavours. The Proverbs 31 woman 'considers a field' in the oldest book, the Bible. You don't need money in your bank account to consider a field. Considering real estate is the starting point, and this is something every woman can do.

As with anything worth doing, if you don't believe it is possible, there's no need to start because your beliefs lead to your action and consequently your outcomes. You can develop the right belief system by getting exposed to the right information. Reading, networking, and seeking out good quality advisors are some ways to gain the right information and build confidence.

It does not matter what state your finances are in or how old you are; it is never too late to start planning, setting goals, and taking the right steps towards investing in real estate. Most of the limitations I've found are in the minds of women.

My very first real estate investment was the purchase of land in Ajah, Lagos. It went bad. Terribly bad. I don't have the plots I bought. I don't have my money back. But I learnt the lessons, and in almost twenty years, I've never repeated the same mistake. Don't let fear of failure kill your dreams. Failure is only failure when you make a mistake and don't get up, unpack it, and learn from it

You have to first of all win the battle over the fear of investing, before harnessing your efforts towards gaining intelligent insight on real estate.

As the saying goes, 'If you think you can, you are right. If you think you can't, you are right.' Be your own biggest, boldest, and bravest cheerleader. It is interesting to note that opportunities only seem to show up when you believe your dreams over your fears. Barbara Cochran, New York's top real estate broker, tweeted this about belief: 'You've got to believe you are deserving of good luck if it's ever going to find you.' I agree with Barbara and love her boldness to bits. You should watch her on *Shark Tank*, the TV show. She's an astute businesswoman and Investor. She understands what it means to be committed to success.

As an investor at any level, you've got to be committed to your own success. Understand that you will make mistakes – even after you become astute. Learn to forgive yourself, and never stop believing. Understand that real estate investment is not for the acrophobic. If you don't like heights and don't like climbing ladders, you're probably going to suffer because the market is dynamic, and change is certain. There's no investment that is 100 per cent guaranteed. Nothing in life is. You've got to get used to the changing dynamics of the market (which happens in cycles) without losing your composure.

However, I've often wondered how women wear those gravity-daring 140-centimetre Louboutin heels (I've only managed to go to 100 centimetres with a lot of pain; okay, I know I'm getting older), but we wear them, and honestly, wearing heels should give us a natural advantage when it comes to climbing the real estate ladder. At least we are closer to the first rung. Another way to view our advantage is that, if we can get around on those scary heels without fear, then surely we can dare to climb onto a ladder that can secure our future. We wear those heels for the fabulousity quotient. I know how many times I've defied the pain of high heels just to be able to strut into a room. The heels make a difference, and we have a strong Why. Most times what stops us from climbing the real estate ladder has to do more with the mindset of fear and not been motivated enough by a strong dream of our future. The real estate ladder goes up, so be ready to go through some steep learning curves.

You can do something only if you have the belief that it can be done. Belief that you're worthy of having a secure financial future with your family will sustain you through the inevitable ups and downs of the real estate cycle. You'll need rock-solid confidence, backed with competent information, that you will achieve success in your investment. It's the same type of solid foundation that you'll need for a good property; the stronger, the better. Belief is a solid building block for investing in real estate. Build belief by joining an investment club with women who have the experience. Women tend to build confidence in communities. Use the power of community to up level your knowledge base and confidence.

B is also for Borrow and for Buy-to-Let. Depending on where you are starting from, how good your credit is, and the type of property you choose to invest in, you may be able to borrow money from the bank at commercial rates, or if you are part of a cooperative at your work place or other investment clubs, you can also borrow through that platform, gaining access to better lending rates. Borrowing to invest in real estate, if done responsibly and with a clear understanding of the implications, affords you the leverage to gain a foothold onto the ladder, especially in a growth market. In my earlier days of investing, because the lending rates were higher in Nigeria and more difficult to access, other female investors and I invested overseas in South Africa just to get onto the buy-to-let real estate ladder. With a small down payment, we secured the properties, mainly studios, one and two beds, and over the twenty-four-month construction period, we increased our deposits to 50 per cent and got a mortgage for the balance over a twenty-year tenor. Some of those properties are still held with a healthy equity, rental cash flow covering the mortgage, and the properties have also appreciated in value, offering the classic twin advantage of real estate investments.

Borrowing in Nigeria is also possible, even with double-digit interest rates. Gaining access to the lower interest rates covered by the Nigerian Mortgage Refinance Corporation through the primary mortgage companies is the best way to go, if starting off and your property is within the threshold. In addition, I've seen some women take advantage of the low interest rates offered by their organisations for home ownership. I advised a few young women recently to take the loans offered by their companies and team up with their spouses to invest jointly in a rental property. At such a low interest rate, compared to commercial rates, it's not savvy to focus on the fear of not being able to repay. The question should be how much can I afford, and how can I hedge my risks?

There are other creative ways to borrow, including what we refer to in Nigeria as instalment payments. As a result of the low mortgage availability and tough lending culture amongst formal financial institutions, most developments and landowners offer an opportunity for buyers to pay over a period of time, usually without any interest. To an extent, the cost of finance has been built into the pricing, but it should not matter to you, as long as the price remains competitive and you gain entry into the investment ladder without the hassle of a formal credit check, as would apply with the banks. This is usually a good way to start, and it's advisable to utilise developer or property owner financing before accessing the usually more expensive and onerous bank financing. Especially for developing countries like Nigeria, where the saving culture and legal enforcement of mortgages are still challenging, the real future will be in finding creative ways to fund and acquire real estate. This should not deter any woman who's serious about getting into the real estate ladder. A good 90 per cent of my female clients have purchased their properties through paying on an instalments basis based on their cash flow. Another developer who's built mainly in Ikoyi and the Lekki area in Lagos shared with me recently that 90 per cent of his clients over the last ten years have been women, and they never default. He said he's had a close to 100 per cent success rate with payments, and in his own words, it's only when the husbands get involved that he's seen some challenges, and typically it's because the men tend to want to bite off more than they can generally afford, relying more on ego than sense. Default rates are very low amongst women.

B is for Buy-to-Let, which remains one of the traditional ways to start a real estate investment. It has many advantages, especially for women and young professionals in the early stage of their careers, with few or no commitments. It can be used as a disciplined project to keep your savings target on track, knowing you'll have a long-term asset that delivers returns over and over. The key advantage of a buy-to-let is cash flow, which we will discuss next.

Buy-to-let means you are investing in the property with the main purpose of renting it to tenants, who will pay you rent for using your property. Some investors focus on options like short-term rentals, long-term rentals, and corporate tenants. Airbnb has made it easier for almost anyone to become a landlord. You can sublet some of your property to people on holidays, especially during Christmas when a lot of Nigerians and Africans in diaspora come back home, and many don't have their own homes. There has recently been a wave of providing short-term, weekly or monthly accommodation for professionals who work in the central business district but commute from distant locations. A gentleman in Lagos has made significant revenues in the billions of naira in Nigeria focusing mainly on this category. Long-term rentals are safer, but there's no harm exploring other options.

C

CASH FLOW, CONTRACTS, COMMISSIONS, CONTROL, AND COMMUNITY

'Every person who invests in well-selected real estate in a growing section of a prosperous community adopts the surest and safest method of becoming independent, for real estate is the basis of wealth.' – Theodore Roosevelt

C is for Cash Flow. Real estate investment becomes a true gold mine if you are disciplined enough to stay focused on your investment from a cash flow point of view. The fee paid by a tenant to an owner (landlord) is referred to as the rent and constitutes your cash flow or income. For an early-stage investor, rental properties are a great starting point, as can be seen from the stories already shared. Cash flow is king and must be positive. It's better to avoid investing in a buy-to-let property where your cash flow is negative; that is, what's left after paying your expenses (e.g., mortgage, if you borrowed money, property maintenance, taxes, and so on). If you did not borrow money, it's still important to pay attention to the lending rate as a benchmark. However, in a double-digit inflation and interest rate economy like Nigeria, it may be sensible to keep your eye on a combination of your cash flow and appreciation as discussed in the earlier chapter. Currently, the average rental yields for typical two- and four-bedrooms in a location like Lagos range from 6 to 10 per cent. I generally won't invest in a property in Nigeria where the yield is not at least 10 per cent, but it takes knowing the ropes, having a clear vision, and staying disciplined. There are three simple ways to significantly increase your rental yield on a buy-to-let investment: if you bought it very early on in an off-plan project (i.e., when you buy from a developer during the construction stage), if you built it yourself saving on the final value of the property, or if you use the power of negotiation through buying at wholesale pricing as a cooperative or community, you could significantly increase your cash flow on an investment.

C is also for Contracts. You make or lose money on real estate based on your contract. If you are educated, you should scrutinise every word in your contract; don't hesitate to get a qualified advisor to assist you professionally. Once you are confident, proceed to sign off so that you don't get into 'scrutiny paralysis.' Get professional help if you're not familiar with what types of documents should be included in the contract. Ensure that you understand the contract terms before you sign.

C is also for Commissions, which can be quite massive when buying or selling property in Nigeria. Remember to factor this into your cost, because they make up a part of the cost of the asset. If you are just starting off, try to avoid or reduce this cost by looking for direct deals, but never play smart with brokers who introduce you to a property. You are better off negotiating with them or asking them to get paid by the vendor/seller, especially in a down market. A good broker will generally be open to supporting first-time investors through reduced or flexible fee terms. Another creative way to manage this is to offer to refer other buyers so that you can get a discount, and if you are really good at selling, you may actually make enough money from referrals to significantly pay for your property. That's one of the ways I started investing in property when I didn't have the down payment.

C is also for Control. The more control you have over a property, the safer it is and the better value you can extract long term. Control refers to your ability to extract as much value as possible in terms of the use of the property, or to utilise the property without undue interference by way of restrictive use terms. It also refers to access to the property in terms of proximity to you. Invest in what you understand how to extract value and in real estate that is in close proximity to where you live, so that you can monitor and manage it when starting off. The farther away you are from your investment property, the riskier it could be. For buy-to-let investments, you can mitigate this risk of distance by researching good quality property managers who will collect rent on your behalf, manage the property, and remit rental income to you. If it's a plot of land, especially when buying community titled and owned land in Nigeria, make sure you've fenced it, and perhaps built a gate house or a small structure. My advice is to prevent undue stress by buying within estates where the title and infrastructure have been taken care of, so that you don't have to deal with hoodlums who may try to prevent you from building.

Control also refers to your ability to enhance your real estate properties without too many restrictions. There are many new subdivisions and cities, such as Banana Island, Orange Island, Eko Atlantic, and Twin Lakes, all in Lagos, and numerous others in big cities like Abuja and Port Harcourt. If you want to extract more value from a single plot, you might be better off buying within a mixed development area, so that you can use it for either residential or commercial, depending on demand. However, as an early-stage investor, you'll need to weigh your options carefully and stay focused on the easy entry, which would typically be single-family residential plots or housing of any kind: apartments, terraces, townhouses, and detached houses. A house has more flexibility for enhancement than, say, an apartment, although you can enhance an apartment to increase its value over and above the others within your block. If you are an advanced investor, you should look at buying plots that you can significantly enhance in future. For example, buying a plot of land in a medium density zone of an estate means that on a thousand-square-metre plot, you may be able to build six to twelve units on the plot, whereas in the low density, you can only build one. It's possible that you may achieve similar returns, but it's usually easier to rent or sell smaller units, plus you achieve a higher rental income over multiple units than for a single large residential property.

C is also for Community. I believe in the power of community; there are many advantages to investing as a community. Successful female investors tend to network actively with other successful investors through work or other opportunities, including female-run investment clubs which tie in with their own investment ethos and appetite. Such groups can provide you with crucial opportunities for networking, education, and support where confidence is lacking. The Finer Wealth Club is a real estate investment club which Fine and Country West Africa set up to encourage female investors to collaboratively invest and take advantage of the power of numbers, shared knowledge and expertise, access to opportunities, and increased confidence. It also helps build accountability and discipline, forcing members to set clear goals, start where they are, save, and invest with a clear vision and a focus on societal good. There's no sense investing just to be rich; we believe that true riches come from the ability to choose in favour of yourself, without constraint of limited finance, and to serve the world with your gifts as you gain mastery of your life and finances. We also like to refer to the good book, the Bible, which says a good man leaves an inheritance for his children's children. We think a good woman can and should do the same. In addition, there may be causes you want to support as you increase your wealth. Giving to causes in various ways is truly living rich, as we see with our role model, the Proverbs 31 woman, who was able to support her household and provide charity.

The most important reason for joining an investment club is for accountability; it offers focus, builds confidence, and gives you access to opportunities that may not necessarily come your way, and at better prices too. I don't personally know of any other formal female investment clubs, but I suspect that with the growth of female networks, in order to add value to members, groups may seek to set up these types of clubs. It's important, however, to ensure that the groups have the right expertise to support members (or at least seek the expertise from qualified advisors). Finer Wealth Club also supports independent groups in setting up and offering the expertise required for actual real estate investments. As with everything, do your homework. Female real estate investment clubs don't necessarily preclude men; it's just that the women are the ones to give access to their families and by doing so are forced to participate in the decisions.

D

DUE DILIGENCE AND DISCOUNTED OR DISTRESSED PROPERTIES

'If you don't have time to do it right, when will you have the time to do it over?' – John Wooden

D is for Due Diligence. Due diligence is a critical non-negotiable factor in real estate. One of the reasons many people are afraid to get on the real estate ladder is that they've heard stories of how someone bought land somewhere and lost it due to omo nile (hoodlum issues in Nigeria). The way forward is to decrease the risk in the property by doing your due diligence.

Due diligence is key. My first real estate adventure many years ago was a disaster. I had pooled together money from family and friends, and we invested in thirty plots of land in Ajah without doing enough due diligence, and relying on a nongovernment-secured title certificate of occupancy. You don't do real estate without ensuring that you have investigated everything necessary, especially title. To cut a long story short, I found myself somewhere inside Lagos, surrounded by chickens and pigs, waiting to see a *baale* (local chief) over land matters. Suffice it to say, it did not end well. It took several years to pay back the family and friends who bought into that project, but I didn't let that stop me. I did bounce back, making $100,000 on a single estate investment on my next deal in 2002. I don't do beast land any more. If it's not secured by government title, I'm personally not interested.

For those who have the appetite, there is a process and a method to investing in beast land, which is my lingo for land where you will have to deal with several human obstacles before you can possess it. Some people have perfected the art. So if you must invest in such places, you will fare better doing so through such trusted companies and schemes, but ensuring they are secured by government title.

'If you don't understand the fundamentals, stay away from it,' Subu Giwa-Amu advised. 'Have a plan and stick to it. I've never had to deal with omo nile. I've had real estate investments. What I have done is to identify good, reputable developers, and I've stuck with them. You find flexible developers who have a lot of off-plan opportunities, and you can make a lot of money doing off-plan properties.'

When you're investing, it's very important to get a trusted advisor on your side. Get a lawyer and check all kinds of government gazettes to know all you can about the property that you're being offered. The Lagos state government, for example, makes a lot of land information available. Get a lawyer to check all the state gazettes and know which family that land has been gazetted to. It's very important.

'If you're buying from a community that's not in the centre of town,' Mrs. Awosika said, 'be closer to the village. You know why? Within that village, they will know. They'll point you to who to talk to, and that will help you.'

Due diligence involves learning how to ask the right questions. Talk to people who have bought in that area before and find out what their experiences were. Check out the families selling the land in that area.

Do not take any detail for granted. Never, ever make any payment to any individual. When you're dealing with a family, ask for a family meeting, which means a gathering of about ten people, so that you can find all the people who are the real signatories, witnesses, and everything. Nowadays, you can even take pictures of the proceedings using your smart devices, as evidence.

You must find a lawyer or estate surveyor who works in that area. They can usually tell you the whole story: who can be trusted, who cannot. This will save you money in the long run.

Also, for those who are risk-averse, the easiest place to start is to buy into what's referred to as government schemes. Enquire from the Ministry of Lands about ongoing schemes at Alausa, Lagos, or other states, get the forms, and apply. There are loads of government schemes right now that aren't even being bought, not just in Lekki but in Badagry, Mowe, and many other places in Lagos and across the country. With government schemes, you cut out a lot of risk because the due diligence has already been done; they're already pre-approved. The bottom line is that whether you do it yourself or not, due diligence must be done. There are also private developers who have already secured all the right approvals and titles. Those are just as good and one of our preferred approaches to purchasing land, especially low-end, low-priced land for early-stage investors. With premium locations, those are usually easier to check, whether already built or plots of land. In every case, a trusted lawyer is your best friend.

D is also for Discounted and Distressed Properties. These are a huge source of wealth if you know what to do. Look out for exceptional opportunities. Every market has them. Seek great deals that offer unprecedented opportunities for capital appreciation.

One of the first transactions I was involved in was a distressed property sale, where the owner owed the bank and was not in a position to pay back. The bank had not yet repossessed the property, giving the owner a window to find a quick buyer, to cover the outstanding loan, plus get a little amount over the loan. The total sale price was ₦35 million. The real value of the property was closer to ₦80 million, but they were under immense pressure and didn't want to risk a foreclosure, where it'd be outside their control plus damage their credit. With other personal reasons that put them in a desperate situation, this was a classic distressed property. It was immediately flipped (resold) to another investor for ₦65 million, leaving them not only margin room, but the property also offered a redevelopment opportunity, as it was located in the middle of Abuja's highbrow Wuse 2, a high-density residential area. That property today, approximately fifteen years later, is worth in excess of ₦450 million. With hindsight, finding a co-investor may have been the best strategy, to hold the property and then develop it, but the goal and focus at the time was to build short-term capital to invest in other similar opportunities and aggressively grow capital, before stabilising cash flow with rental income and long-term properties. Your vision drives your investment strategies and decisions. Stay focused but be ready to adapt if you know better. However, there's never any need to regret; the best attitude is that there are always new and better deals ahead. Strive Masiyiwa, a top capitalist and mentor, mentioned this investment principle in his recent Entrepreneurs Town Hall meeting in Lagos: 'never regret.' It serves no useful function. You can't do all the deals that exist in the world.

Please be warned that these types of deals that I described above don't happen every day; they require an in-depth knowledge of market values and a quick sense of intelligent marketing so that you are able to sell off. Your strategy is to flip it quickly; have patience if you want to get it right, and be disciplined to keep looking for only truly distressed deals, if that's your preferred type of investment. Not all deals will have these types of margins, and truth is you shouldn't look for those levels; a good 30 to 50 per cent below market in an economy like Nigeria is a good start.

E

EQUITY

'Real estate investing, even on a very small scale, remains a tried and true means of building an individual's cash flow and wealth.' – Robert Kiyosaki

E is for Equity. Equity is your best friend. If you borrow money to invest, be sure you have enough down payment, referred to as equity. Depending on your long-term financial objectives, you could generally start off with higher equity contributions and look to reduce your contributions over time as you become more confident. The more equity you have in a property, though, the safer your portfolio.

Typically in developing countries like Nigeria, where access to mortgages is very limited, your equity requirement is high, ranging from 30 to 50 per cent and in some cases more. When investing overseas in, say, the UK or the United States, if you have good credit, you can borrow with very little down payment. Your down payment or deposit on a property is referred to as your equity. In addition, when the property value rises, the increase becomes part of your equity, after the cost of repaying the loan amount.

Most investors, especially at an early stage in Nigeria, will have a lot of equity in their homes, because they aren't comfortable with borrowing to invest, or it could be a case where the property may have been inherited. Some may have paid fully and own the property outright. In any of these cases, there's an opportunity to extract equity from the property in future to invest in an additional asset. Extracting equity is essentially getting a loan using the unencumbered value of your property. To do this, however, you have to demonstrate to the bank that you have a source of repaying the money borrowed against your property.

A simple formula to adopt is, the higher your equity, the lower your risk and the safer your investment.

F

FINANCE AND FINANCIAL DISCIPLINE

'She considers a field and buys it: From her earnings she plants a vineyard' (Proverbs 31:16).

F is for Finance. When starting out, consider using savings from your salary or other business proceeds, like the Proverbs 31 woman. You can start saving towards investing in real estate today, regardless of the economic downturn. Just make sure you stay true to your agenda and don't get sidetracked.

Banking expert and personal finance coach Nimi Akinkugbe said that this is the best time to create incredible wealth in Nigeria, because stocks are at rock-bottom prices, and real estate prices are also on the soft side. 'Even if you've missed the boat this time, don't let it happen to you again. This cycle will happen again. The next time this happens, make sure you have the cash to buy the stocks and property.

'It all comes from saving,' she emphasised. 'Saving constantly.' She has a plan to own property, to live in a nice place, and to be able to support her husband in the education of their children. So she saves a set amount of money every month, whether she's broke or otherwise. It goes by direct debit into the stock market every month. 'So my real estate has come from stock market investment and saving,' she said.

It's about discipline and consistency. That's what gets you the savings you need to invest in real estate. Pick a particular amount to save every month, and stick to it.

In terms of access to financing, banks and financial institutions are increasingly recognising that finance is a doorway to empowering women and that female entrepreneurs offer an especially attractive opportunity. So they are providing products targeted at women.

However, many of these products are ill-conceived and mismatched to the reality of most entrepreneurial or professional women. In addition, the cost of financing remains a major source of discouragement for women, who generally tend to be more conservative. There is definitely a need for property developers and financiers to get more creative so as to tap into the ingenuity and commitment of an increasing army of women who are rising up in the marketplace.

If you already own real estate, you should be aware that owning property makes it easier to own more. Once you get a home or other property, financing subsequent projects gets easier. The banks will usually ask what property you already own.

Finance is key, and how you fund your deal makes a huge difference. There are many ways, including mortgages (which are seldom used in Nigeria), short-term loans, and developer finance (otherwise known as off-plan payments).

An off-plan project is a property you buy before it has been constructed or while under construction. You can buy a property at different stages of completion. If you bought it before it's been built, then you've bought an off-plan property.

There are a few advantages and disadvantages of investing in an off-plan project. One key advantage, if you do your homework, is that it will most definitely appreciate over construction, as you would have taken some risk with the developer and therefore bought typically at a price below market versus a completed property. You can also pay in stages and, in some cases, according to your cash flow. On the other hand, a key disadvantage is the uncertainty; construction timelines change, and sometimes, the promised quality isn't delivered. However, these are all risks that can be mitigated.

There are other sophisticated approaches to funding your real estate investment when cash is low, including joint ventures (JVs), which we'll look at later.

I'm often asked, 'Is it best to invest in the outskirts of major cities if you have very limited funds?'

Sadly, low income earners actually pay a higher price per square metre for their rental property, so you might find better yields outside the city centre because most people are uncomfortable with dealing with people of a certain class.

That notwithstanding, you could become the astute landlord of low income earners, providing them decent accommodation. One good way to maximise your funds is to partner with others to buy land and take your time building as your income comes in. Partnering or collaborating also gives you negotiating power, like the cooperatives have, and acts as a source of increasing funding.

Nimi Akinkugbe bought her first property through an investment club she started with her sister and two other friends, because she didn't have enough money on her own. They each had ₦1.5 million, and four of them pooled their funds together and bought property worth ₦6 million at Abijo (where she never even visited). Money spoils friendships, as they say, so the terms were laid out very clearly, and they knew how many years they wanted to hold it before they sold.

They sold it four years later for about ₦22 million, and she thinks maybe they shouldn't have, because it's worth more than that now.

What are the costs to look out for? Acquiring real estate in Nigeria is very expensive. Costs could range from 10 to 20 per cent, which includes agents' fees, registration of title fees, mortgage registration fees, interest (if financed), and so on, but there are ways to reduce some of these, especially if you're part of a cooperative group or investment club. Government fees, however, are fixed.

One key finance consideration your advisor should be able to help you with is whether you should take a loan for an investment property. Does it make sense to take a loan with interest rate in double digits (approximately 18 to 21 per cent per annum)?

Annual rental income from residential properties is in single digits, typically ranging from 5 to 8 per cent of the property value. When you are borrowing money to invest in homes, your total return (rental plus appreciation) should, as a rule, exceed the interest that you are paying. This is very difficult to assess in a dynamic market. Nevertheless, with the right strategies, you can achieve a successful outcome if you look long term and buy the right properties under the right terms.

The key thing is this: don't let finance stop you. Start by educating yourself through reading and attending real estate workshops. These are some financial pitfalls to avoid:

- poor planning in the ability to manage cost projections
- matching the wrong financing products with the right project
- lacking discipline in applying funds strictly to the purpose allocated

This brings us to another F: Financial Discipline. This is perhaps the most critical element of success. Real estate is generally a mid- to long-term play, and financial discipline requires investors to not only save for a rainy day, but sometimes sacrifice designer shoes or jewellery for a brighter future, an area that many women have a challenge handling. Ibukun Awosika once shared the story of a woman who started putting aside 10 per cent of the housekeeping allowance her husband gave her and eventually saved ₦10 million.

She also has this to say: 'It's really about how you approach building the future for yourself. It's about, I always say, don't eat your dinner for breakfast. Why is that important? There has to be a season where you strategically make sacrifices towards a season where you can go to sleep. My head office is called House of His Glory; I bought the land for ₦13.2 million. That's Lekki 1, and it's the main commercial line officially in the Lekki master plan. I bought it for ₦13.2 million in February 2000. Three months later, plots like that were about ₦30 million, and obviously you don't want to ask how much it is now. It's the discipline not to consume at the most critical span of your working life that guarantees that you can build continuous wealth. Because you see, the wealth that you build will definitely continue to generate wealth for you, especially when seasons change.'

Financial discipline requires choosing not to do some things, so that you are able to do other things later. Sometimes, you have to make an inconvenient decision in favour of your long-term vision. For Mrs. Awosika, it was choosing not to buy a car, which is a liability and not an asset. Instead, she chose to hire taxis and their drivers. 'By the time I bought my first brand-new car, I had built House of His Glory,' she said.

In addition, as traditional nurturers, many women tend to put the needs of others ahead of theirs. Many give up their financial nest eggs for the privilege of helping desperate spouses, children, and relatives, without realising how this impacts their long-term emotional and financial well-being. As far as playing the caregiver/nurturer role is concerned, balance is required.

'Most of our mothers were not financially strong on their own or independent,' Mrs. Awosika noted. 'Though they were major contributors to what their husbands called their assets, they weren't even careful enough to make sure that those assets had their own names on them at all. They worked very hard, joined everything with their husband. Some worked to pay for the guy to go to school; he got the degree but considered it his own instead of a joint asset; because once you part funded it, the education itself became your joint asset, and in turning the asset of the education into value, the man will take all the value to himself. All the extra wives can come out now, and he can even write a will that does not include you. So when you look at the way our mothers have lived, it's a totally different generation. The reality is, we are in a different time. Unfortunately, we are careless. The reality is that times have changed. Eight out of every ten women that you know are working very hard and are major contributors to their families. There are many women who are the ones building the family, and there are many women who are raising children by themselves. One thing I always say to challenge the heart and mind of a woman, is to understand that building personal wealth is a responsibility; it's not a choice. Husbands die, fathers die, men lose jobs, things happen, and overnight what seems like a stable home, sustained by somebody else's sweat, is put at risk because the other partner is not a major value contributor.'

Even if your spouse is well off, you still need to learn financial discipline and be a value creator.

'The times and seasons that we are in, I don't see many men today that can on their own carry the load, because of the kind of costs that are involved now,' Mrs. Awosika continued. 'If you have kids in England and up to last year your husband was able to pay for it alone, he probably is struggling right now. Right now, you need more than his income because the cost has multiplied.'

I'm going back to the fundamentals to make you understand why it is important for you to be a major value creator. Being a value creator, you have to be a wealth builder for your household. You must earn respect in your home, and it's about what you bring to the table. Because what are you: a net liability or a net asset in your home? And it's also not about consuming everything that you generate, which is another major mindset based on the first mindset, because you think somebody else is taking care of it, so you can consume. Now, the issue is you actually get to the point where your husband despises you. Why? Because he's working so hard to pay the bills, pay the rent, pay children's school fees, and he sees new bags and new clothes walking into the house every day. And 'Oh, I lost a tire yesterday; can you make sure they fix my tire?' That's you. 'Oh, the bulb is out; you need to call that guy to fix the bulb. Oh, your brother said he's doing something; you better make sure you send money to him.' Or 'My father needs this; I need your help to do this.' No.

You need to get to a point where before you're even asked, you have the value that you add. And I always say to women, it's easier when you make the choice of where you want to play than being forced to play it. So it's easier for you to say, 'Guy, you know what? I think we need to start investing in properties. You know, building a house or something. I will feed us until we finish this house.' And you control it, so you can control the cost and your expenditure. But what you've just said is, no more housekeeping.'

And she would know, having practiced this for decades.

'I remember that it was two years into our marriage and we were going to start building,' she recalled. 'We bought our first plot of land somewhere by Chevron. We were going to start building, and I said to him, "Okay, you face the house; I'll take care of the home." We've been married for what? December this year, it will be twenty-six years, and for the last twenty-four years, I've never asked for money for us to eat. At that point I just said, "I'll face this, you face that," and that's how it started.'

Financial discipline is non-negotiable for a woman who wants to build the future. Get started today.

G

GOALS AND GUIDELINES

'Owning a home is a keystone to wealth: both financial affluence and emotional security.' – Suze Orman

G is for goals and guidelines; these two go hand-in-hand.

When investing in real estate, as with life and business, it's important to determine your goals and guidelines for each investment. You must have a clear investment objective before you put your savings in any investment, but this is especially true for real estate, whether residential or commercial. Different people invest for different reasons. Be clear what you are buying and how you intend to derive value from it.

Secondly, ask, what can I do with this property? What uses can I put it to? Can I subsequently expand the use? Thirdly, will it yield good returns commensurate to my investment? Fourthly, will it grow steadily over time?

Setting your goals should include the following considerations, amongst others:

- Residential versus Commercial (shops, offices, hotels, and properties typically for public use)

The choice between residential and commercial properties depends on availability of money and your investment objective. Commercial properties typically generate regular income from business users through rentals, while residential properties offer more appreciation benefits and rental income from individuals. When you're just starting, residential is clearly a good place to cut your teeth because most people buy their first real estate to live in.

- Built Property versus Land

I am often asked, 'Should I buy land or a building? What are the advantages of each?'

There is no one-size-fits-all answer to this. It depends on your goals, your resources, and where you are in life at that point in time. I remember decades ago, when my husband first tried to buy a house in Nigeria. Having just returned to the country, he was still thinking in terms of mortgage, so when we found a house we liked, he asked the sellers, 'What are the terms?'

They went, 'Huh? What terms?' We soon realised we were better off buying land and building.

Land rarely generates income, although it can be put to good uses pending when it is built. However, land gives you flexibility to express yourself and maximise your investment.

Any developer will tell you how land prices are skyrocketing. Investing in land is always good for long-term investment, especially when you want to avoid maintenance costs. Plots tend to give higher returns, especially in Nigeria.

On the other hand, a building is usually more restrictive in terms of varying the use of configuration, but you can generally earn an ongoing income quicker. So while land can be part of your real estate portfolio for capital growth and future expansion, a building gives you immediate income. Angela Aneke often emphasises this. And she knows this first-hand, having invested in real estate in Ghana, Nigeria, and South Africa.

Her investment in South Africa was an opportunity I brought to her attention and guided her through. We not only convinced her of the wisdom of investing in the two-bedroom house in Sandton, we also advised her to furnish it, since furnished apartments rent faster. It indeed attracted a great tenant very quickly, and it's exciting to know that this property paid its own mortgage every month. The house essentially kept paying for itself until she sold it for a profit.

Nimi Akinkugbe had a similar experience. 'The best thing I've ever done is in Ghana,' she said. 'Very easy, over four years off-plan.' She bought that property by selling stocks at a high. The property has been let permanently, and with money from her rent in Ghana, she set up her company, Bestman Games.

She worked in a South African bank, and she realised that South Africans were buying land in Zimbabwe. So now she's looking at major property going for low prices there.

In fact, your building can continue to appreciate in value over the years, serve your interests, bring in rent from tenants, and still serve as collateral when you need it to. Ibukun Awosika buttressed this point.

'I always say to women, especially if building businesses, you need to build assets on your own that you can use to create value for your business. Now there's no bank you're going to go to that's not going to ask you for some form of collateral or the other. It's a property need, a good collateral.' She further explained, 'The same property that you can use as collateral for a loan is also generating rent for you. So you have two streams of income from the same asset, at the same time.'

At some point, you should begin to look at investing in real estate as an asset for your business.

It's good when you tie your business to asset building. Once the business is doing well, that cash flow supports the real estate. For instance, most people see MacDonald's as a food business, but it is more than that. It's one of the biggest property businesses in the world, because it always looks for prime locations when it comes to positioning the business. If you buy property for your business using a mortgage plan, it can pay for itself from the proceeds of the business, and eventually you own the property. Also you can lease and plan to own the property.

Your goals also determine what sort of real estate and locations you should be looking at. If you are interested in cash flow, then you have various options, from apartments and single-family homes to retail shops. Really almost any location is viable to a large extent, if you do it right. Wherever there are people, real estate is needed. Studying the market and knowing what's required in that location will make that location the right one for you. If you are looking to grow capital, then investing in distressed properties, very low priced properties with strong growth potential, is the way to go, but you must understand the market and be disciplined about your decisions.

Identifying emerging locations is a learned discipline which anyone can become great at if willing to commit the time and effort. An example was one my first successful investments, a property that was priced at well below market. To recognise property that is below market price, you must first know what market price is.

Things are changing in Lagos. The Lekki axis is the fastest growth node in Nigeria, but it also pays to look at places like Epe, Isheri, and Ikorodu.

Places that seemed like the end of the world in those days are no longer so, and people who buy when the land is cheap enjoy the benefits later.

'Sokoa Factory sits on two acres plus of land,' Ibukun Awosika said. 'My husband bought the first acre for ₦2500 years back. He said someone just took him there, and he said, "Okay, I will buy." It looked like useless land by the sea, in a village nobody was ever going to come to. So he bought, and his friend bought. Many years later, when he knew that I would never go to Ikorodu [to set up my factory], he said to me, "You know what? I know you. That Ikorodu, you will not go there. Let me go and show you somewhere I think will be more useful for your factory." So he took me there.

'I needed more land, and by the time I was buying, the villagers sold it to me at ₦150,000 per plot. This was 2004. Now, the free trade zone has come right opposite us. So every plot in that area is anything between ₦5 and ₦10 million per plot. So my total factory land is two acres plus a little extra, and two acres is about twelve plots, so we're sitting on about thirteen plots, one portion of which was bought for ₦2,500 by my husband, who was wise to buy, and the rest was ₦150,000 to me. Do the math from just 2004 till now, and think of the value.'

Your goals must include your exit strategy, as well. It's also important to be clear upfront when you intend to sell. The answers to these questions should form your guidelines and will save you a lot of time and money. Be clear on your investment tenure, as real estate typically takes some time to dispose of. You must match your objectives with your strategy.

Decide clearly on what you want to accomplish, and be very specific. Then commit to taking one step forward and then another.

H

HOLD

'Buy on the fringe and wait. Buy land near a growing city! Buy real estate when other people want to sell. Hold what you buy.' – John Jacob Astor

H is for Hold. Being able to hold property is vital. Knowing which properties to hold and which to sell, when to sell, or when to hold, is an art and a science. You get real value from some assets when you sell them off at the right time. A friend of mine bought property in Victoria Garden City at ₦18 million and held it for six years before selling at ₦65 million.

Subu Giwa-Amu's father invested seriously in property. However, he was always very quick to sell. 'I said to myself that I will not do the same thing,' she told me. 'I will hold on to property. So as much as possible when you get on to the property ladder, you need to hold on, stay on. It's not the rental income that makes you big; it's the capital appreciation from the property.'

A clear understanding of the times and seasons vis-à-vis your goals is key to making the right decision. When in doubt, refer to your goals. Real estate is generally better played as a mid- to long-term holding game for the best value to be extracted.

Time matters when it comes to the hold position.

Time is generally your best friend. If you want to make the most amount of money in real estate, then buy and hold for as long as possible. In most economies, especially in high-growth locations, property prices tend to double every five to seven years, which means that you should look at a minimum of five-year strategy to realise good growth.

Timing is key, particularly for investors who have a short- or medium-term strategy. If, however, your strategy is long term, then your timing is not as important. The gold strategy should always be to make as much money as you can when you buy, which means buying the best value property you can.

Even though market timing is important and plays a big part in turning a good property deal into a star, I personally believe that there's never a bad time to buy property. How many people wish they bought into Lekki 1 in Lagos, which started at ₦2 million and is now N₦150 million, or Banana Island, which started at ₦7 million and is ₦400 million about twenty years later. I recall buying a plot of land for a client in Banana Island for about ₦35 million in 2006, and practically forcing him, kicking and screaming, to buy two plots because he had received a bonus, and I didn't want him to pass up on a fast-growing location. He sold one plot for approximately ₦150 million about three years later and built two houses on the other plot with the money he received.

There are cycles of high-growth spurts which aren't always replicated. Ultimately, being in control of one's financial future entails knowing not only when and where to buy, but also when to sell. It's a decision that should be based on your personal circumstances at the time; most importantly, market conditions can change your game plan. Stay flexible. Be careful, though, not to move in or out of property at the wrong time of the cycle without good advice, as nothing is ever fail safe.

I

INSURANCE

'People who live in glass houses should take
out insurance.' – Anonymous

I is for insurance.

One of my favourite Nigerian songs is Fire Fire or FIA by popular mega music star Davido. The chorus gets me singing at the top of my voice-
"Yeehh! I love you, no mean say, if you say make I put one hand for Fire
Fire Fire burn them
I go put hand for Fire ooh
E no mean say, if you say make I put one leg for Fire
Fire Fire burn them
I go put leg for Fire ooh"

I recall dancing to this song on repeat on a girls weekend getaway to Accra, Ghana, and for some reason that song just never seemed to leave my head.

A few months before that weekend trip, my son who was seven at the time had woken me up at just past midnight, because a fire had broken out in his room. My husband had travelled overseas just that evening, and I recall telling my son Kenelum to sleep in my room as a treat (I intended to stop allowing him sleep in my room when he turned eight). He however for some strange reason refused to sleep in my room and insisted on sleeping in his room. It turns out this was a fortunate thing as I was later woken up with a loud, 'mummy, mummy there's fire in my room'.

Confused, I ran to his room, and saw flames making its way towards his bed. He ran for the door to go get help, pointing out that we had a fire extinguisher- mummy use it while I go and call the security guys downstairs, he said.

Sadly I had no clue how to operate the fire extinguisher. Instead I called the building manger who immediately sent a maintenance team, who managed to put out the fire with the fire extinguisher. The fire station was also alerted. Fortunately, we suffered minimal loss, and got away mainly with strong heart beats, some charred furniture, burnt books and great memories of little man Kenelum being a hero for staying calm through out the incident. My fertile imagination however got me thinking that evening about what sort of insurance we had in place and what it would have covered. Would it cover the property and all the content that may have been destroyed?

The general concept of insurance was born out of the need to protect against and manage risk. Essentially. insurance serves to restore you financially in the event of an unexpected loss. It requires you to pay certain amounts to the insurance company usually on a fixed term, and be assured that they will bear the cost of any future loss you suffer in accordance with the terms of your policy.

Taking out insurance on a property will provide protection against the most key risks to your property, such as fire, theft and some weather damage. There are some specialised forms of property insurance which include, building insurance, content insurance, fire insurance, flood insurance and earthquake insurance. Don't make assumptions about what is covered. When in doubt, ask for specifics. For women especially, it is important to know that your expensive jewellery and vintage handbags or other personal effects, may require additional cover as part of content insurance if it's a property you occupy.

Your insurance policy should outline clearly what will be paid for and what will not be paid for, so be sure to read the contract carefully and know what is covered. Always read the fine prints. Yeah yeah! I know it's boring... (rolls eyes) but at least keep it safe.

With the benefit of hindsight, I know that it's one joyful reality to dance to Davido's song, singing at the top of my lungs, fire, fire burn them, and quite another horrifying reality when you wake up to behold real fire in your home in the middle of the night when the last thing you expected was fire. But that's the point, no one plans for an accident. However, smart investors protect themselves against it, should it occur.

A real estate investment is one of the biggest and most expensive you will ever make. It's wisdom to ensure you are properly insured.
You can't do without insurance when investing in real estate. It would be kobo wise, Naira foolish or to say it in Queen's English, penny wise, pound foolish to try to avoid getting the right insurance for your properties.

J

JOINT VENTURE

> 'There have been few things in my life which have had a more genial effect on my mind than the possession of a piece of land.' – Harriet Martineau

J is for Joint Venture (JV). If you think investing in property is beyond your reach, then it might be time to think about joint ventures.

Thanks to joint venture partners, you are able to accelerate the growth of your real estate portfolio and achieve your goals much sooner than if you were to do it alone.

There are a number of reasons to engage in a joint venture when it comes to real estate investment, but mostly because you lack the expertise, the network, the time, the borrowing capacity, or a sizeable deposit to do your next property deal.

It is also important to note that a joint venture enables you to get into bigger deals. For instance, you may have a piece of land but have no money to develop it, so to extract value from it, your only option may be to sell the land. However, if you find a friend, family member, or investor who could provide the funding or even an architect or construction company that's willing to partner with you to develop the property, you now have a bigger pie. By having a joint venture, you may be able to build a block of apartments instead of having to sell the land.

It's is also possible to come together with partners, friends, and colleagues to jointly invest in a bigger real estate deal; you could end up with a lot more profit than if you are to buy individually.

When it comes to negotiating joint ventures, make sure you find the right partner with similar investment values as you. Everything and anything is negotiable. A lot will depend on the circumstances of the parties investing and what each party brings to the table. The person who owns the property and holds the title may not have the financial resources to make a deal happen. In some cases, they won't want to make a deal; you may have to acquire the property from them and co-own it with other investors.

Financial partners provide the cash/equity/financing for a stake in the deal or an agreed interest rate or return.

Loan partners are responsible for raising a bank loan and paying interest. Some people have great credit and can access better terms to fund a transaction, using their existing collateral, either a property or other assets. They may also already have an existing pre-approved line of credit that can fast-track your project.

Project managers contribute time and generally find and manage the transaction to completion.

It is important to agree upfront on the underlying strategy for the project. How will you split the profits, who pays for what, when, and how will it be disbursed? Some investment approaches include the following:

- Short term flip: Sell and split the profits as agreed.

- Long-term buy and hold with a clear future exit plan, timelines, return levels, and so on. It could also include one party buying out the other at an agreed value.
- Jointly develop multiple units and split the titles, with each party taking their portion of the project.

These are some of the important things a joint venture agreement has to include:

- What are the responsibilities of each party?
- What is the exit strategy? What is the end goal or termination point of the JV?
- How will equity and profits be split?
- How and when will profits be paid out? If there's a loss, will it be split?
- How will you deal with death, divorce, illness?
- Who will handle the disposal of the sale?
- How will tax be dealt with? What structure will the JV be structured in?
- Who is responsible for accounting?
- How will disputes be resolved? Who is responsible for making transaction decisions if there's a disagreement?
- What sort of contingency plan and financial buffers are required to ensure the investment succeeds?

As you can see, co-venturing is not to be taken lightly but has very significant upsides. I have personally participated in some great joint ventures, which has helped to build my portfolio, but I also suffered from some downright terrible ones. I can confidently say that the defining factor is the person you go into the relationship with. Entering into a joint venture is a bit like a marriage, and the character of your partner is the single most important factor. I found this out eleven years ago when one of my partners in a joint venture deal tried to take over an investment I had created. Once he found out that I was ill, he immediately tried to take over the project, claiming that he contributed funds to it, but what he forgot was there was more to the project than just cash contributions. It is very important to ensure that irrespective of the relationship or your judgement of the parties, you properly document your contracts and ensure they are legally binding.

In Nigeria, the joint venture route to investing has become a major approach to doing real estate deals at all levels. Women are coming together and investing in collaborative groups, sometimes through a cooperative or investment club. Some friends are buying plots of land and building their family homes together to maximise the land and reduce cost. Others are approaching property owners and negotiating to help them find financial partners and put together a development team to build large projects that the owner may not have the capacity, competence, or resources to undertake alone. Building trust with stakeholders is an important part of creating joint ventures, and this is an area where women are uniquely gifted, as they tend to approach negotiations from a win-win approach, which helps to build trust.

If you have land or property, you may want to consider a JV to improve the value. If you can't fund an investment fully, look for partners to share the opportunity with. If you are new to real estate or trying to gain confidence, don't just think about affordability. Instead, think collaboration. The partnership could be structured as a one-off or maintained for ongoing deals. You can look for land, organise the expertise, assemble the team, develop other resources, and manage the project for a stake in the profits. That's a major leg onto the real estate ladder. It's higher stake but comes with higher rewards.

Subu Giwa-Amu said, 'You could start in small multiples. Even if it's a shop. You could get a group of friends and co-own.' She also said she had to sacrifice over the years. She didn't take out the rent from these properties. Instead, she invested it in subsequent projects with developers, getting in at an early stage. She went into property, she said, because she was looking at her family's financial future. She knew there would come a time when seasons changed. That was her driving force for going into real estate.

'We have to be disciplined as women,' she said. 'Some women would say, "*Subu Ijebu,*" but the time will come when I can buy ten Chanel bags if I want to. It's not a priority.'

You don't have to be the owner. You can get into real estate as a tenant and still optimise the property, bringing in other investors or sub-tenants as a way of getting into a better and bigger property than you can afford alone. That's what Giwa-Amu did for her current property, located in South West Ikoyi.

A different angle for joint ventures is to consider using the power of brokering a deal by tapping into your networks and collaborating to get onto the real estate ladder. One of my real estate mentors, Pam Golding, a leading developer of luxury South African real estate, started through introducing properties to others, and this was how I started as well, leveraging my network of friends and family to introduce transactions for them; you can either earn a fee or get a stake in the project. It doesn't even have to be a business. Most women have extensive networks and can do this quite productively. If you hear of a property and refer someone to it, and they buy, you can approach the agent, landlord, or developer with an offer to pay you for bringing in that investor. There's no law that says you can't earn a fee. That's what got me onto the property ladder, through referrals and the power of networks and collaboration. Think joint venture; think, *How can I add value to the process of a real estate transaction?*

K

KNOWLEDGE AND KEEPING TRACK

'The best investment on earth is earth.' – Louis Glickman

K is for Knowledge. "An investment in knowledge always pays the best interest," Benjamin Franklin said. And in Plato's words, "Human behaviour flows from three main sources: desire, emotion, and knowledge."

Knowledge is key in real estate. You must seek it. There are risks and opportunities, but the first thing is a strong desire to create a secure financial future, which leads to seeking the right knowledge.

To successfully invest, the starting point is research, gaining a basic understanding of the area you are interested in developing knowledge. Before I ventured into real estate, I was practicing law in Lagos and also owned the Zanzibar Art Gallery, which initially began by selling imported pottery from Accra, Ghana, paintings, and crafts from my home, generally to friends at social get-togethers. I subsequently expanded it to reach beyond my friends, moving into a small twenty-square-metre space within a shopping centre on Victoria Island. But it was really always a hobby rather than a serious business. One day, someone gave me a copy of *Nothing Down* by Robert Allen, also author of *Creating Wealth*. This book about how to invest in real estate when you have no money; it changed my mentality and created a strong desire to look into real estate, which I had started getting exposed to as I placed my art pieces and pottery in various homes in Lagos.

One of the big lessons I learnt from the book was the importance of researching your neighbourhood; you must research the opportunity, gain a deep understanding of the fundamentals of the investment, and learn how to spot a good deal. It was truly an incredible eye-opener which ignited my appetite to invest successfully in real states. I subsequently closed my first few transactions on the back of the knowledge gained from reading Bob Allen's books; I started attending real estate investment seminars wherever I could find them, travelling several times to the UK, Dubai, and even South Africa, just to learn how to invest in real estate. Today, you don't need to travel; there are numerous online resources, webinars, and podcasts; local companies, such as our Fine and Country West Africa, offer investment seminars and resources to help people get the knowledge they need to get started.

All types of investments require knowledge. The more knowledge you have about the opportunities that exist, with an understanding of the risks and how to mitigate them, the higher the likelihood of success. Knowledge helps you identify low-hanging fruits and helps you interpret the times and their implication on real estate investments.

Lack of financial knowledge is a stumbling block. An inability to interpret the market will affect your success. Be aware of the economic indicators and get clued in through seminars, reading the news, researching, and joining investment clubs.

Get knowledge, and by all means, get understanding. In real estate, you must know your numbers. Know your location. Knowledge will always give you an advantage. It will also give you confidence, and you need to be confident to succeed in real estate. Access to the right information increases confidence, which keeps you from being bound by analysis paralysis and prevents knee-jerk responses to every fly-by-night opportunity. That's why this book has been placed in your hands: to give you knowledge, information, and insight so that you can gain confidence and take advantage of the opportunities that real estate presents in an emerging economy.

K is also for Keeping Track. Keep track of every document related to your interest in property. This is critical and cannot be overemphasised. Knowing where your title documents are, when your title expires, what the taxes and other obligations are, and other aspects of your transaction are all your responsibility. If you are not sure what to do, seek legal support. I can't tell you how many women don't know where the title documents of their homes are. It's not unusual for African women, including sophisticated, professional women, to feel uneasy about wanting to discuss this with their spouses, fearing they will be labelled ambitious or charged with having an ulterior motive. It's actually shows a lack of intelligence and personal irresponsibility to own a property and not know where the title documents are, whose name is on it, or how safe it is. Some women have been in situations where they thought they owned a property, only to find out that the property belonged to a bank, relative, or close friend.

In a particularly unfortunate case, a lady in her late fifties recounted to me how she had invested in a property with her spouse; in actual fact, she bought it and fully paid for it but thought both their names should be on the title. She left him to arrange the legal aspects and never followed up. Sadly, she was subsequently dispossessed of the property when they ended up in a contentious divorce. I am mindful in writing an investment book for women not to bash men or make them the culprit. My focus is to make women more accountable to their financial future, recognising that life happens, and in situations not as dramatic as this, there's a responsibility to organise your title documents and conduct a review every now and again.

L

LAND

'Buy land; they're not making it anymore.' – Mark Twain

L is for Land. I like to say, land is one of the scarcest commodities, but in response to the Mark Twain quote above, Nigeria is making land out of the sea: new islands are being created by filling lagoons on Eko Atlantic, Banana Island, and Orange Island, but even with this, land is extremely limited in relation to the population of Lagos. Land is always a great investment in emerging economies like Nigeria. We are a developing economy, and this means we have incredible opportunities; people need to be housed, and hospitals and medical centres are needed, as are schools, hotels, and shopping centres. Many of the challenges we have are actually significant opportunities. I don't like the terms *underdeveloped* or *third world*, but the word *developing* excites me, and it should excite you too.

By 2050, Nigeria is looking at a projected population of three hundred million people, so I want you to recognise that the population itself is the biggest opportunity for real estate in this country. Will you be the one to acquire land that will create themed parks, housing for senior citizens, university housing, retail shops, or business parks?

Unlike in other developed countries, acquiring land in Nigeria is usually a great way to start out in real estate; many people start this way because of the low entry price point compared to an existing property. If you have some savings for investment, buy land and start building while still living in a rented property. You can take your time to build as you increase your capital or go into a joint venture development with financial investors. The rate of appreciation in land in Nigeria is very high and tends to outstrip inflation, making it a good means of hedging and also protecting your long-term savings.

Mrs. Awosika shared with me something her father taught her about land: 'He said once you have land, you have a house. I've never forgotten that, because the way he explained it to me as a young woman is, all you have to do is look at the land and say to yourself, what do I have to do first? If the first thing I need to do is dig the foundation, look for the money to dig the hole. Once you see the hole, excitement will force you to ask, what next? They will tell you, they do blinding. Then you'll find out what it costs to blind. That's just cement and water. Then you'll ask them, how many blocks do I need to start coming up? Buy the first five hundred, the next thousand; once you do that, you'll find that you start to come up. Before you say Jack Robinson, you're at a place where nobody can sell you *asoebi*; for what? You're building. Once you have the colour, wear it, and if they will not accept you and your colour, don't go. There's no problem. When you finish building, they will come and celebrate with you.'

Investing in underdeveloped land is always cheaper. Also, with land, even if you do nothing, your land still appreciates. Another story from Ibukun Awosika illustrated this:

'In 2004, in order to set up my Sokoa Chair Centre factory in a joint venture with some French investors, I had to put down a capital of 75 million naira as my own contribution. And this was a time when government policy had sort of shut us down as a business. I told my staff to calm down. I remembered that in 2000, I bought eight plots of land just before Chevron, and the cost came to about ₦5.2 million. When I needed 75 million to put down as capital, I decided I wanted to sell that land. Remember, I bought in 2000. In 2004, I sold it for ₦61.7 million. I did nothing; I didn't even build a fence. I didn't put a stone down. Nothing. Because that family in particular, their land is very secure. So in this case, all I had was the deed of assignment from the family because they had the master certificate of occupancy. I sold it once I put it on the market.'

Two people can own a plot of land and extract different levels of value from it. For instance, if you buy land, you can lease it to a farmer or to a telecommunications company, until such a time as you are ready to develop it or sell it. Yet another story by Mrs. Awosika resonated:

'In 2005, I went to Ikorodu when I was trying to build this factory; someone said there was plenty of and in Ikorodu. So I went and bought six plots here, two acres there, and eight plots there, and they were all between ₦250,000 and ₦300,000 per plot. I didn't do anything. I gave one of the six to the church for an orphanage they were building in Ikorodu, so that was a seed which I would get the harvest. Then on the two acres, I'm building an estate which we're just finishing, twenty houses. So the other eight plots, I just decided, you know that Ikorodu was too far for me; I couldn't even get there. I don't go there; somebody goes to see the property and sends me pictures and videos of what's going on here, the development and all that, because the traffic there can drive you crazy, but the investment ... This is another thing: People think they need to buy where they like. It's not about you; it's an investment. So it's not about you want to build the kind of houses you want to live in. No.'

Fast-forward a decade later, and the beauty of investing in land becomes amazingly clear:

'See that other eight plots I was talking about? I was sitting down at Christian Missionary Fund a few weeks ago, before the ball, and they asked me for a large sum of money towards the ball. I was sitting there, thinking I was so low on cash right now, and someone called me and said, "Are you willing to sell that land in Ikorodu?" I said, "Yes, make me an offer." This was someone I knew well. He's the guy who took me there, and he's always looked out for the land.

'So I said, "Make me an offer." And he said, "What if I pay you three million for every plot?"

'I bought it at 400,000. I've never been there; I can't even identify where it is: that's the honest truth, but the guy knows where it is. One of my staff told me it was worth about 5 million. I knew that, because I already checked. But you know what? This was the guy that kept that land for me; I've never been there. And he's a pastor, so I consider the rest of it a seed.

'I said to him, "It's fine; you can pay me that price, as long as you can give me the money tomorrow morning. Because I'm at Christian Missionary Fund right now, and they need money."

'So he said to me, "I can give you this much tomorrow morning."

'I said, "Done deal."'

The point I'm making is this: when you learn to create value, you won't even know at what point it will become valuable to you. The honest truth is, if I never got value from that land, it would have done nothing to me because it was an abandoned investment. It was ₦400,000 × eight plots, ₦3.2 million, which I paid eleven years ago. I don't know the place; I don't even know the land, but at a point of need, it showed value, value that was tangible and useful for my purpose. So when you're talking about someone using their property to solve a medical issue, the reality is I would have spent that ₦3.2 million and not even remember what I did with it so far back. Or the ₦5.2 million that I paid to the *kabiyesi* and three years after or so, I got ₦61.7 million.'

Another reason I personally advocate investing in land is that it gives you more options. You can subdivide the plot of land, build on one part to rent out and live in the other. You can do pretty much anything, as long as you build within the code.

In my experience, though, I advise women to buy land within schemes that have less risk, that is, where title documents are secure and you don't have to deal with baales and omo niles. Those things can derail you.

Also, pay attention to location. Location, location, location, they say, and with good reason. What makes a great location generally includes good infrastructure and quality demographics. However, in a country like Nigeria, emerging pockets with high but good quality density could work out to be a good location when looking for high yields and growth. Understanding development trends is an important factor for success. Depending on its location, land, arguably, has a higher appreciation percentage than built-up properties, certainly in Lagos, according to our research at Fine and Country.

M

MORTGAGES AND MANAGEMENT

MORTGAGES.
"While I encourage people to save 100% down for a home, a mortgage is the one debt that I don't frown upon." Dave Ramsey

M is for Mortgages.
Mortgages are basically a form of loan typically from a financial institution where you borrow money to buy a house and pay interest on the loan. The most important thing to be clear about when considering a mortgage, is how you intend to pay for the principal amount borrowed and the interest charged on it.

As discussed under B for Borrowing, in developed economies, mortgages are the key options for financing a property acquisition. To determine whether you should get a mortgage and what type of mortgage it's important to understand some basic information about mortgages.

PAYING BACK THE INTEREST
There are a few options for making interest payments - fixed rate and variable rate mortgages are typical, while capped rates are also options. With the fixed rate mortgage, your rate remains the same over a fixed

period typically 2-5years and this helps you plan better, but you may not be able to exit without penalties and you will not benefit from a reduction of interest rates, but these are rarely used in Nigeria because of the economic volatility. They however help with budgeting especially if interest rates are likely to keep rising. The variable interest rate is more commonly used in Nigeria and it's important to note that this could expose you to unilateral interest rate hikes from the lending institution whenever there's a change in rates or for whatever other reason they decide. The Capped interest rates puts a ceiling on the interest rate you pay, but will be reduced if rates fall. This is also a great option for budgeting if available.

PAYING BACK THE CAPITAL.
You can have either an interest only versus a repayment mortgage.

The interest only mortgage typically helps you manage your cash flow for a short period of time by reducing the monthly payments to only the interest due with a balloon payment to be made at a specified future date. It's typically used by investors who intend to flip a property or in some cases where a short term financing tenor is required because the borrower has a guaranteed source of paying the capital at the future date. The repayment mortgage requires a combination of your interest and capital to be repaid typically monthly and is typically higher but reduces the loan much faster.

The Loan To Value (LTV) is also an important factor in accessing a loan. It represents the ratio of equity contribution you will be required to make towards the property. Typically, in more developed economies, you could contribute as low as 5-10%, a 90-90% LTV for Residential mortgages, whereas in Nigeria as with other developing countries, buyers could be required to contribute as much as 30-50% making it extremely difficult to get the initial deposits.

As usual you should always negotiate all the key terms and ensure they work within your financial capacity.

My real life experience with what I refer to as a 'quasi mortgage' facility in Nigeria was frustrating because it was nearly impossible to track the interest rates or understand the calculations which seemed to change quite frequently. As a more experienced investor, I kept the loan for as long as it served my interest to do so, but I couldn't wait to pay off the bank loan as soon as I was in a position to do so. The day I did, represents one of the happiest days of my life, and yet I am grateful that I could access that loan at the time I did as it made the difference between been able to own that particular property in the initial stages.

Contrast that to my more stressless experience of obtaining and maintaining mortgages in more developed countries, with single digit interest rates and much longer loan tenors, giving you room for easier payments and healthier returns, and a better experience. Mortgages continue to represent the single most frustrating yet powerful opportunity for real estate investing and economic growth in developing countries.

Some key considerations in taking a mortgage should include: 1. How much financial risk are you willing to take?
2.) What can you afford to pay taking into account your current and future financial obligations. 3.) Do you want a short or long term mortgage? Typical tenors are 10,15, 20 or 25. Some are up to 30 and depend on the age of the applicant.

4. How often do you want to make the payments? Quarterly or monthly? In rare cases, you may be able to negotiate bi-annually to tie in with your cash flow.
5. What is the maximum deposit you can afford to put into the property? This will determine the loan to value. Generally, higher LTVs lead to higher interest rates, because they are seen as riskier for lenders. If you put down say 80%, you should be able to attract a lower interest rate than someone who put down 10 or 20% as equity. In addition, the lower your deposit, the higher your repayment.

You certainly don't want so much money going towards your mortgage payment, that you can't afford to enjoy a life or have enough for other obligations, or investments. It is also important to prioritise your mortgage payments as your property can be repossessed if you fail to keep up payments.

It is important to note that inspite of the potential pitfalls of obtaining and maintaining a mortgage, there are advantages to having a mortgage on a property all things being equal. Specifically, it enables you gain access to properties without the need to have all of the funds personally. The power of leverage also works in your favour by increasing your return on actual cash invested especially if you intend to sell the property at some point. If you obtained a buy to let mortgage, it's beneficial especially if your rent and other expenses are significantly lower than your mortgage. There are also tax benefits to mortgages but be sure to get professional advice.

The real power of real estate in Nigeria will not be unlocked until mortgage financing at sensible interest rates and for long tenures are in place. This is one of the fastest ways to build the wealth of nations. Sadly mortgages are still very scarce in Nigeria as in most developing countries, and the interest rates extremely high, creating a challenge for the housing market and the overall economy.

> 'Land monopoly is not only monopoly, but it is by far the greatest of monopolies; it is a perpetual monopoly, and it is the mother of all other forms of monopoly.' – Winston Churchill

M is for Management. Good quality management makes the difference to your asset. Look out for properties that are well maintained and that have transparent processes in place. Also be clear upfront about the management fees and be sure you can afford it in the long and short run. As a result of recession in the last two years, many investors are extremely sensitive to the question of service charges, and rightfully so.

In Nigeria, if your investment is a buy-to-let, tenants generally pay for most of the facilities management and service fees. It's important, though, to factor this in for periods when you have no tenants. Some women tend to have an advantage when it comes to maintaining their properties, often beautifying them and ensuring that they have what in real estate is referred to as kerb appeal or the wow factor. Many years ago, Uzo Nwani bought a one-bedroom property from our company as a buy-to-let investment; her property rarely has any vacancies, because tenants always preferred her apartment when they came to inspect the available units. The simple reason was that after every tenant moved out, she invested time and resources to do a light refurbishment, paint, change wallpaper, and do any repairs, clearly giving her an advantage over other investors who don't care. The truth is that your personal standards of cleanliness and maintenance should come through in your properties, whether owner occupied or rented. Ultimately, it comes home to roost and makes sense if by maintaining your property in a state of good repair, you reduce your void periods. Be careful, however, not to overcapitalise; watch the costs and maintain a low-budget, high-value approach when maintaining an investment property.

As a business, facilities management presents a massive opportunity in the real estate space that remains largely untapped; it's quite suitable for women to consider investing in, if they have the competence and passion for managing and maintaining property. The field covers property management services, which is generally more client relations, and the more technical maintenance, which you could hire, go into a technical services agreement, or subcontract and provide general management.

Anyone who is able to crack this area of real estate, even when it comes to managing your own properties, will have an edge. A well-maintained property will always have a pricing advantage.

N

NEGOTIATION

'Landlords grow rich in their sleep.' – John Stuart Mill

N is for Negotiation. Negotiate everything. It's that simple and that important. Buying well is buying early and negotiating properly. Negotiation is your best friend in real estate transactions. To negotiate intelligently, you need access to the right information, so get it. Women haggle even when it doesn't count for their future. We negotiate over little things in the market, sweating the small stuff. In real estate, what you're actually buying is the level of your negotiation. You make money in real estate at the point you buy, not when you sell, so negotiate where it matters.

In the words of Angela Aneke, 'Don't only think about when you buy the real estate; think about when you sell it too. Be as meticulous when you sell as when you buy.'

The best investors never buy at market price, ever. They never pay full asking price or make full payment upfront unless there's a significant upside. When buying off-plan, particularly in Nigeria or other high-growth locations, look to lock in the value and then allow appreciation to be your friend over time while you offer low deposits and pay the balance in instalments. Get good advisors to give you the power of knowledge. Arm yourself with the right information, and negotiate a good deal.

Here are a few tips for getting the best when negotiating a real estate transaction:

- Never be in a hurry.
- Do your research and know the right price point. If it exceeds your threshold, walk away.
- Cash is king and puts you in a good position to negotiate. The higher your deposit, the more likely you will get a better-than-average discount. Always get a cash discount.
- Leverage the power of numbers to get a discount. Buy in bulk with friends and colleagues or as part of a cooperative.

When buying property, you buy terms not the property. Understand the most critical terms for your circumstance, and make that your benchmark for negotiating; for example, is price more important than level of reservation deposit? Is the timeline for making the payment important? Is the finishing being offered at an acceptable standard, or can you ask for an upgrade?

Your ability to close quickly is also an advantage you can use to negotiate a deal. If you don't have to sell something to make the investment, or if you have a pre-approved line of funding, or if you don't need many layers of approvals from other parties to close a deal, you are generally in a position to get the seller to offer a more acceptable price if they know you are willing, capable, and ready.

As much as it is important to research and get opinions, don't get info analysis paralysis, which women tend to suffer from, second-guessing themselves and sometimes losing confidence. If in doubt, consult with a competent real estate advisor (not just your lawyer or banker, because sometimes, they are too conservative and not as savvy about the commercial aspects).

O

OBSERVE GROWTH PATTERNS

'Don't buy the house; buy the neighbourhood.' – Russian proverb

O is for Observe. Observe the neighbourhood you want to invest in. Do your homework when buying an investment property, especially buy-to-let. Visit during the day, at night, on weekends, and on weekdays. Ask questions of everyone, including security personnel, local businesses, and residents. Understand if it's a growing location or a dwindling location. Is the neighbourhood changing? How is it changing? How will it impact your investment? Is it becoming more retail, increasing in density, or attracting a different resident pool? Some of the fundamental things to check out include the demand versus supply in a particular neighbourhood, which will impact rental and occupancy levels. Be observant.

Look out for areas that offer high economic potential and future growth, often referred to as the 'path of growth.'

In particular, land in emerging areas (in the pathway of infrastructure and population growth) has an especially high potential to go from undesirable to desirable; this offers really high returns in the long term for investors willing to wait.

Paul Onwuanibe, CEO of Landmark Group Africa, discussed this at a Refined Investor Series hosted recently in London by Fine and Country West Africa, in collaboration with *BusinessDay*. Onwuanibe said, 'Identify a path of growth, and go there before everyone else gets there.' He described their acquisition of what has now become a strategic and iconic piece of real estate in Lagos, at a time when there were no roads or major infrastructure. The property has clear water views and is now considered a prime location, with major players opening up retail spaces, offices, and hospitality and residential projects.

It is also important to discover whether locations or estates have restrictions on the number of buildings to be built or where land is limited for building, as this translates to higher demand for what's available and creates exclusivity, which impacts future values.

In a place like Lagos, fundamental shifts, like the development of the Free Trade Zone, the Lekki Sea Port, the Lekki Airport, and various industrial, residential, and mixed-use developments can open up the potential of a location and many connecting sublocations.

The returns seen across the board in numerous residential estates across Lagos (from Ajah to Epe, Lekki 1 and 2, gated estates like Twin Lakes, Banana Island, Parkview, Osborne 1 and 2, and other far-flung areas) bear anecdotal and research-based evidence to the desirability and potential of land investment as the proverbial golden egg. I believe it's a real golden opportunity if you choose properly and manage the acquisition process effectively. This makes land banking a strong option for families looking to diversify and hedge their risks as part of their retirement or education investment plan.

P

PRIME LOCATION

'I have always liked real estate, farmland, pastureland, timberland, and city property. I have had experience with all of them. I guess I just naturally like the good Earth, the foundation of all our wealth.' – Jesse H Jones

P is for Prime Location. These properties are like blue-chip investments and generally make great returns in the long term. Prime locations are typically areas that have a solid reputation for attracting top-tier companies, especially multinational and high-net-worth clients. Some of the factors that determine how prime a neighbourhood is include safety, quality of infrastructure, organisation, and density.

Prime locations in developing countries will typically have the foreign missions and embassies, top corporations, and captains of industry, and of course they command higher rates both for sale and when it comes to renting. Many investors at this level started at the lower rung of the ladder and gradually scaled up to becoming owners of prime real estate. It doesn't happen overnight and has its unique set of challenges, including higher holding costs for vacant periods. The recent recession in Nigeria hit a lot of owners of prime real estate very hard, with many properties remaining vacant for more than a year and in some cases for more than two years. However, the trick for investors at this level is to adjust their mindsets and recognise that the market has changed; they must be quick to adapt their pricing and expectations. The challenge for most investors is when they haven't planned or factored in the holding cost for void periods. Real estate can be very tough in tough times, but when it rebounds, it usually makes up for the losses.

On the flip side, downtimes offer a great opportunity for investors to gain access to prime real estate that may otherwise be elusive because there are many more properties on the market, and sellers are more flexible. Recently, some of our clients gained access to prime Ikoyi properties at almost 50 per cent below the historic prices. It took showing them that for similar prices in the not-as-prime location of Lekki, they could get onto the more upmarket Ikoyi ladder. Many investors don't realise that they should include in their search locations and properties that are seemingly out of their affordability range; the trick is to ask how you can find the discounted deals within these neighbourhoods.

Recently, an old client shared a story about how he had bought a property at the height of the real estate downturn. Less than a year later, when the market started regaining momentum, he had a property that was essentially worth three times what he paid; he received numerous offers but refused to sell, subsequently building his dream home on the two-acre property in a choice part of Ikoyi. In future, this investor will extract more layers of value from the same property by developing a multiunit luxury apartment block. Even in today's sluggish real estate market, you'd be hard placed to find that same sort of value in a similar location. His story is not unique. Investors understand that money is made during tough market times. We have definitely seen an increase in investors specifically looking for discounted properties. Where better to find these than the prime residential market in Ikoyi and Victoria Island, where many sellers are getting more realistic?

No money for prime real estate? No worry. Get creative with financing. Here are three quick tips if you are thinking of looking at prime property opportunities but don't have enough immediate cash:

Flexible Payment Terms: Remember that real estate investment is really about terms. Are you able to close quickly, or do you want to put a deposit and negotiate a longer time to pay (in some cases, without incurring interest, whether for off-plan or already completed properties). Don't be afraid to ask questions. Get the best payment terms possible. Use your credibility and cash flow to secure great deals if you are absolutely certain that the deal is significantly below market.

Cash: Remember that cash is king. Your ability to conclude with full payment upfront could make a massive difference to the discount you get. Sometimes, you may have enough for a property outside your budget, by offering a massive payment upfront or full payment in a situation where the seller may need cash in a hurry, especially with new residential developments.

Partner/Leverage: Remember that you may not have all the cash, but you could partner with other investors to take advantage of discounted properties, if the opportunity is truly great. You might even consider a bank loan if your future cash flow supports it and the opportunity is exceptionally great.

How else can you climb onto this rung? Start by referrals, if necessary, to build your cash deposits, if you can't afford to get on the prime ladder yet. Remember also that you can buy the smallest unit, even a one-bedroom within a prime neighbourhood, as a step into this much-coveted ladder. Another interesting thing to note is there are sublocations within locations. Some roads in Ikoyi are better positioned and attract a higher value than others. Banana Island and Old Ikoyi still command a premium over Parkview, Osborne, or Southwest Ikoyi. Within Ikeja, the Government Reserve Area, old colonial locations which used to be reserved for the top government officials, commands a higher value. Within Lekki, the waterfront and the high street which can be converted to commercial use command a premium than the areas towards the second Lekki gate. Some locations are more prime within a prime location. And some specific real estate developments can become prime locations because of the nature and scale of the project and the impact it has on the lifestyle of a neighbourhood. Victoria Garden City, Nicon Town, Carlton Gate, and the recent and much coveted Twin Lakes (although located in the not-so-prime Lekki Ajah axis in Lagos) command a premium over other properties in the same location due to their scale and lifestyle features. Eko Atlantic City is also priced significantly above Victoria Island prices because of its infrastructure and new city category. Some of the best value and growth opportunities may be to buy in the lower priced sublocations within a prime location.

Q

QUESTIONS

'The art and science of asking questions is the
source of all knowledge.' – Thomas Berger

Q is for Questions. Questions are your best friends in real estate transactions. You can never be lost if you ask questions. You don't ever want to be the party in the dark. Ask lots and lots and lots of questions, and then do your research. It's better to be safe than sorry.

When buying into a residential or commercial development, the old adage that real estate is all about 'location, location, location' is no longer enough, so at Fine and Country, we now rely on the five Ws of real estate, especially in off-plan projects, which are common in developing countries.

By asking the following (and other) questions, you can future-proof your investments:

Who? When buying into a new construction project, ask who the developer is. It's important to know who is behind the development; do they have a track record of completion, or is it their first time? The same applies for the contractor. Will the building be completed on time and to the stated quality? It extends also to the future management. Who will manage the property?

What? What is actually being developed? The development must be relevant to the market and its location in order to raise finance and not end up as an abandoned project. The development should have the relevant facilities required by its target market. Knowing what's being built will help you assess the risk of completion and delivery. You obviously want to make sure others will find value and buy so that the project is viable and gets delivered. Some developers tend to cut corners on low-profit projects.

For example, a development describing itself as luxury should have at a minimum basic lifestyle amenities such as a pool and gym to justify the asking price. Luxury, of course, should go beyond basic amenities and should typically offer features that create a sense of exclusivity and desirability that regular buyers would aspire to. Luxury is after all about a sense of pride and accomplishment more than anything else.

When? When will the development be delivered? Is the stated time frame realistic for completion? Are there any penalties on the developer for late delivery? Successful real estate investment and development is all about timing.

Where? Where is the development located? Location is more than just its immediate surroundings. Important location considerations include the area's security; access to transportation hubs; and proximity to good schools, hospitals, restaurants, and leisure centres.

Wow? Does the development have the wow factor, that something special that sets it apart from the competition? This can be a combination of many things, from extraordinary views such as Lakowe Golf Estate and Asokoro Gardens Abuja, defining water features such as the man-made Twin Lakes by Chevron, to the use of technology and distinctive architecture, such as in Eden Heights, Victoria Island, and the Azuri in Eko Atlantic City. Adding these types of features not only attracts initial buyers, it also underwrites the value of your investment long term. Iconic projects speak for themselves, create enhanced return on investment, and retain their value long term as they are easier to rent and resell, which in turn impacts your returns. Learn to ask questions and be meticulous about cross-checking the answers.

R

REFERRALS AND REPUTATION

'It's all about people. It's about networking and being nice to people and not burning any bridges.' – Mike Davidson

R is for Referrals. Referrals to your network is a great way to start building your much-needed capital to invest in real estate. When you create value for your network by referring good real estate transactions to them, you can often earn a referral fee from the seller (unless you are an acquisition agent).

The Power Brokers Circle, which was recently launched in Lagos by Fine and Country West Africa, is a good platform to join if you want to create passive income through referrals. Women tend to spend more time socialising on social media, but you can turn this influence amongst your friends, fans, and colleagues to real estate capital by combining socialising with a purposeful approach to creating referrals. They'll even thank you for it.

Do your homework, however, before referring friends and family to properties. Preferably work only with tried and tested brands.

R is also for Reputation, which is everything. Reputable vendors, advisors, and tenants are your best insurance against erosion of value. Be willing to pay the price, where necessary, for this peace of mind. Your reputation as a landlord is also an asset in attracting the right tenants or buyers. Imagine owning a property in 1004 Estates in Victoria Island. Imagine that several hundred landlords have apartments to rent at the same time. Tenants will prefer renting from the landlords who have well-kept properties and attend to their clients in a professional manner. Tenants also tend to prefer dealing with landlords who are represented by trusted professionals rather than having to deal up close and personal with the landlords themselves. In some cases, especially as a start-up property owner, you may want to manage and deal with tenants directly, but try to keep it as professional and objective as possible. And definitely get proper contracts in place. People can tell when you are trying to cut corners.

S

SOLUTIONS AND STRATEGIES

'Buy real estate in areas where the path exists ... and buy more real estate where there is no path, but you can create your own.' – David Waronker

S is for Solutions. Creatively solving housing, office, or retail spaces and other real estate problems is the true value that real estate brings. 'There are lots of empty houses between Ikoyi and Lekki,' Ibukun Awosika explained. 'So, the rich people are already full, but we still have a massive population of people. It's a mindset. It's how you think about holding value. It's how you think about adding value. There's holding value, and there's adding value. It's how you think about building assets for the future.'

In real estate, it is best to start small. As Subu Giwa-Amu put it, take bite-sized pieces for a start. When you start, start simple. Begin with upcoming areas, and then grow from there. House people first; it's a basic need. People are crying out for affordable housing. Nigeria requires seventeen to twenty million housing units to address its housing deficit, and that could be you creating solutions to address this need.

You can also help your children become landlords, whether they're schooling in Nigeria or abroad. A law student at Abuja Law School built twenty one-bedroom apartments there, and they're all fully let to fellow students.

You must learn how to see yourself as offering significant value to the economy as an investor. The way you view your investment makes a difference as to how you treat it and what demands you make on it. Serious investors see themselves as solving problems, for which they are entitled to get paid properly and on time.

S is also for Strategies. With real estate, you create wealth in two main ways: through real estate appreciation and through cash flow (rental income).

Real estate has several benefits and solves several problems, including the following:

- diversification
- appreciation in value
- a hedge against inflation
- ability to influence performance
- retirement savings option

However, strategy is vital in extracting these benefits. Two major considerations in real estate investment are the fact that it requires management and the costs of acquiring and selling properties. Without strategy, it is impossible to get the best out of real estate.

Here are some real estate investment strategies:

- buy land and hold for capital appreciation
- buy wholesale and sell retail
- fix up, upgrade, and rent or sell
- develop new buildings for sale

- develop new buildings to rent
- buy retail and hold to rent
- acquire bank-repossessed properties

'You don't have to love the place you're buying,' Nimi Akinkugbe said. When she wanted to invest in a property in Elephant and Castle, her husband and children said, 'What? Who's going to go there?' Yet that's the kind of diversification that's critical, instead of putting all your eggs in one basket. It was right next to the underground, right next to the British Rail, and it was an opportunity visible to the astute eye. In the fifteen years since they bought it, at a time when it was easy to do because the area was rather dodgy back then, it has proved to be a valuable investment. It's been let every single day since they bought it.

As an owner-occupier, you can also be a landlord by letting out some of your underutilised spaces. In Nigeria, we need to start building more of what South Africans call 'granny flats,' essentially extra space outside the main house, what we call guest houses but which are rarely used.

When I was in law school, I lived in the service quarters in my uncle's building. I didn't call it a BQ then; I called it a pied-à-terre. Years later, when I had one of our first offices, we had service rooms that young graduates paid rent to live in.

How much redundancy do we have in our homes? Strategy is key to unlocking value.

Will communal living, house shares, or fractional ownership be the future for real estate ownership for millennials? Who will create the structure to make this easier for younger investors to get onto the ladder? Will they need smaller, more convenient types of properties? The bigger the problem you solve, the better your returns.

T

TITLE AND TERMS

'I would give a thousand furlongs of sea for an acre of barren ground.' – Shakespeare

T is for Title: Title documents are critical. Without them, you do not own anything. For us at Fine and Country, title is everything. As an investor embarking on your first real estate investment (and every one after that), look out for this. Good title is critical because if you don't have a title, you don't have a property. Just as you won't go to a university and come out without a certificate, you wouldn't buy a property without ensuring you have the right title. Take time to be detailed, and tidy up.

T is also for Terms. Terms make all the difference. In actual fact, you don't buy real estate; you buy terms. The structure of your contract terms could make a significant difference to your returns. Learn the hidden trade secrets for structuring investments profitably.

Some of them will include payment terms, negotiating extras to be included in the property you are buying, ensuring that you get the right guarantees, and even putting conditions to when payments are due. Make sure you get a good real estate negotiator on your side when acquiring a property. They could make a significant difference to your returns. When I started investing in real estate, some of the most important factors for me personally included getting low deposits, flexible payment terms, long timelines to make the payments due, and tying those to my cash flow. For me, it made the difference to whether I was able to get on the property ladder or not. To this day, I believe the lower the deposit I initially put down on a property to secure it, the better my chances are of making the decision and commitment. Once the deposit is made, you find that you will stop at nothing to ensure that you make it happen. All of a sudden, all your unnecessary purchases and financial distractions go out of the window because your money now has a focused mission.

Another important issue to watch out for is to make sure you have an exit strategy that is not costly. Some contracts have high costs of cancellation or transfer to a third party should you decide to exit before completion. Watch out for these types of restrictions, especially if your intention is to make a short-term return by flipping the property (selling it quickly for capital growth).

U

UNDERSTANDING

'Nothing in life is to be feared, it is only to be understood. Now is the time to understand more, so that we may fear less.' – Marie Curie

U is for Understanding: To be successful in real estate, always seek to understand what exactly you are going into before you sign on the dotted line. Never be afraid of saying, 'Could you go over that again, please? I don't understand it yet.' There is no shame in inquiring repeatedly until you understand.

As an investor, it's important for you to understand the full context of the challenges so you can reduce the risks and come up with ways of addressing them.

Understand the terms of your contract before you sign. Understand the market cycles. Understand the times and seasons you are in. Understand your personal finances. Understand your target clientele in whatever type of real estate investment you need to make. Get knowledge, and by all means, get understanding. If you're considering lifestyle development, understand the challenges facing lifestyle developers such as access and terms for funding, risk management (currency volatility), infrastructural challenges, and regulatory bottlenecks. Understand the matrices and policies that will change the playing field of real estate.

You should also understand why you are buying. Every now and then, I get asked, why is real estate so expensive? Does it even make sense to buy when you can rent? Real estate is expensive, but it need not be if you are armed with the right information. Expensive means you are not getting value for money. If you know the market, you should not buy expensive. Depending on how long you want to live in a location, it may make better sense to rent rather than buy. Typical rule of thumb is that if you will live there for a minimum seven years, then you should consider buying. Real estate cycles have been known to run in seven-year cycles, but there's no real proof this is still valid in all locations.

'Wisdom is the principal thing; therefore get wisdom: and with all thy getting get understanding.' This great biblical advice is also relevant to real estate.

V

VALUATION AND VALUE

'Real estate is an imperishable asset, ever increasing in value. It is the most solid security that human ingenuity has devised. It is the basis of all security and about the only indestructible security.' – Russell Sage

V is for Valuation: This is key to your being able to create wealth from existing real estate. Protect your wealth by ensuring your valuations are up to date.

The concept of revaluing a property is similar to that of rebasing an economy. Imagine that you have owned a piece of real estate in your family for more than fifty years, and the last time it was assessed, it was worth ten shillings. However, the economy has changed. The currency has changed. The real estate market has changed dramatically. There are many investors looking for your type of real estate, and in addition, the approach adopted in valuing your real estate has changed. So much has happened, and yet your asset is still carrying the same valuation in your mind and on your books.

One day, a trusted advisor brings to your attention that you are actually living in the past, with an asset worth more than you recognise. You call in a registered valuer, who assesses and confirms that your property is now worth $1 billion. Wow, you think. But wait a minute. What does that mean? You still have the same sprawling old house on several acres of land, but not much else has changed. Your bank balance is still the same. You still feel as limited or as cash strapped as you felt before the valuation.

Before you go off the deep end, thinking this is voodoo, your trusted advisor educates you further. Your real estate has been revalued and assessed at its proper worth, but it is all potential until you unlock the value. Potential? Real estate? Unlock value? How, you ask.

There are many ways to unlock value. You could knock the house down, redevelop the property, sell it, or lease it to someone who wants such a property and is willing to pay the right value. You could get a bank to finance all of these approaches, using your revalued asset. Irrespective, all of a sudden, you are now in a better position, both with the banks and even psychologically, knowing you have all this to your credit. A whole new world of opportunities suddenly opens up. However, you still have to get the right advice and act to extract the maximum value from it.

When the real economic value is measured, local and international investors will go beyond eyeing the opportunities and start taking real action. And that could make things get really interesting. We haven't even scratched the surface in Nigerian real estate, whether it be commercial, residential, retail, hospitality, or specialised real estate, whether in the low, middle, or premium segment.

It's better to undertake the valuation yourself before it's required. If you use reputable values, the bank's valuation is unlikely to deviate too far. If it does, you can dispute it and ensure that they arrive at a sensible one. We once disputed a valuation done for our client by a bank that was going to give her a mortgage. The bank's valuer underassessed the property, and we insisted on getting a second valuation, which we did get and which made a difference to her loan terms.

V is also for Value. Once you invest right, value is guaranteed. At least, even when the market goes down, you only lose, or crystallize your loss, if you sell at that moment. If you don't, the value is retained, and after a while, the market will pick up again. And at that point, you're still collecting rent, so you're really not losing. Real estate always has value.

Several factors affect the perception of your property's value. Even your words can confer value on your property or strip it of value. For instance, developing a property and calling it a compound house does not inspire confidence because the word *compound* does not represent value for Nigerians.

At the end of the day, people pay for perceived value. The words you use, the name of the property, or the way your property looks affects how people perceive its value.

If you're a real estate investor, having an astute eye often comes into play. Investors who know their onions would recognise value in a property even if it's in need of a coat of paint or has bedsheets hanging around it or hasn't been designed as best as it could. That investor will go in, price it at its devalued rate, and then upgrade it for value. When you buy the most perfect property, there's less value for you to unlock. Go for the ones that have room for you to add value and earn more. You can turn a property into double what you paid for it. The person who can see the beauty in a property when it doesn't look pretty is the person who can get the most out of it. You can find or add value in any property in Ibeju Lekki, Mowe, Benin, or Abeokuta, not just in Ikoyi.

Here are three ways to unlock value in your current property:

1. Oversized homes: Are you still living in an oversized home that could benefit from remodelling? Conversion is a good opportunity if you have a big property in a good location. Simply convert the use. When you solve a higher level problem, you get higher returns.

It may be possible to turn your existing home into a mini residential project. Does it have more land than you currently require? More rooms than necessary? Children gone off to school or married? You could consider scaling down or restructuring your residence to extract more value.

When all my children but one went off to school, we realised one day that in a six-bedroom house, we were all living in only one room. With just one child at home, did we really need all that space? We made a decision to downsize and unlock the value of the property by redeveloping or selling it.

Could your current house become a block of apartments or a few terrace houses? To create more value, in some cases, depending on the location, furnished apartments do better.

Beyond housing, other options abound. For instance, retail is huge now. When it comes to retail, we only just got going in Nigeria. You may want to consider malls, so it's good to look at just one part of the current statistics:

In Nigeria, there is one mall for every 1.5 million persons.

In South Africa, there is one mall for every fifty-four persons.

Needless to say, opportunities abound in retail. If your house is on a major street, you can even consider a small shopping complex if the zoning regulations permit. You could also convert your house to a hotel or an office, subject to zoning laws. A few homeowners on major roads in Lekki have gone down this route. Once again, it's important to emphasise that you need to go through the proper regulatory process to get approvals for a change of use.

Conversion is not about how big it is. It's about doing it well. Make it pretty, solid, and attractive, and you will reap great returns on your investment.

However, if you're converting with the aim of positioning for the luxury market, the rules are different.

Firstly, good quality doesn't cut it. If it's good quality alone you have to offer, then it's not luxury. Good product quality is not enough. Iconic quality is the target, with an unsurpassed commitment to craftsmanship, as seen in some of the visionary developments in Fine and Country's portfolio, such as Asokoro Gardens, Abuja, Centre Heights Residences, Victoria Island, Civic Centre Commercial Towers, the award-winning Osborne Towers, Ikoyi, and Eden Heights. A swimming pool and gym do not necessarily create luxury in a development. Luxury developers have to go beyond providing basic amenities; they must offer features and services that exceed the core needs of the target clients.

Hermes has consistently invested in crafting a compelling story of mystique and successfully sold the storyline that Hermes does not just sell leather goods. In my opinion, the Hermes brand presents clients with coveted access to an iconic lifestyle.

This resonates with our belief at Fine and Country that luxury real estate is not about brick and mortar but about intelligent solutions to complex high-level needs of discerning clients.

Furthermore, if it has to be sold, it's not luxury. Luxury is not touted or sold with desperation. Luxury is delicately and artfully presented in a manner that creates the sort of mystique and desire that true luxury brands have mastered. Product functionality is rarely presented in selling luxury products. At Hermes, all consultants go through an orientation called 'Inside the Orange Box' where they are indoctrinated on how to assess and indulge their target clients' desires.

Desperation, on the other hand, does not sell luxury, and nothing spells desperation like multiple salespeople competing to push a product. If you have to push it, then it is not luxury. Luxury is selective. Luxury is patient. Luxury has tradition, sophistication, and excellence embedded into every aspect of its process.

It is also important to note that scarcity is a strong marketing strategy. Scarcity creates desire, which is the strongest marketing approach for a luxury brand. Desire attracts a premium price (in some cases, it commands an irrational price, unrelated to cost or other factors).

The recent marketing approach adopted by Chevron Pension Fund in presenting the exclusive Twin Lakes estate in Lekki is consistent with the sort of exacting standards top brands go through. In Nigeria, however, very few developers of high-end real estate are that patient or astute, possibly because of a combination of the high cost of financing projects, a lack of sophistication, and an awareness of what it takes to create long-term value for a development brand. This is an area that Fine and Country has specialised in and has provided support to some of the leading developers in the luxury segment with consistently positive results.

2. Equity release: Most people have gold around them in the form of equity in their homes, which they probably bought or built with cash. Of course, you must have a solid way of repaying the loan. Getting an equity release is a good way to raise capital for additional real estate investments or even for investing in other ventures.

3. Sell: Sell and move into a smaller property. Selling your current home may be the wise thing to do if it has ceased to serve the purpose for which it was originally conceived. You could sell up or sell down. Selling down means divesting for the purpose of investing in a smaller property; this approach releases much-needed cash which you could invest in another income-producing property or another type of assets to create a balanced portfolio, depending on where you are in your investment cycle. Selling up means selling your current property to invest in a different property (usually in a different location that costs more). This generally comes with a change of lifestyle and status and is considered more as a lifestyle investment rather than an astute investment.

The same goes for building a house in your village; is it considered an investment or asset? The simple answer is, it's a lifestyle asset, not a bankable asset. However, this depends on what infrastructure exists around your village and whether you were reasonable in building it to suit your needs versus overcapitalising. If you can afford its maintenance from other sources of income, then it's fine. If you can extract other value from it, that works, as well. Some people rent space in their village home to a telecommunications company or create boutique guest houses.

W

WAITING

'Don't wait to buy real estate; buy real estate and wait.' – T Harv Eker

W is for Waiting: Buying well is buying early, not waiting for perfect timing, since real estate generally tends to benefit from long timelines. Although caution is critical in real estate investment, fear that leads to paralysis will affect your success in all areas of investment and curtail your financial future. The best time to start investing in real estate is as soon as you can afford it, and this is even more so when the economy is down and the market has practically ground to a halt, because then you have the power of negotiation.

Real estate is always a long-term play; the longer you have, the better your outcome. In fact, one important reason to start investing in real estate early is future appreciation. It helps to have years ahead of you.

'Your future flows are also important when it comes to financing real estate,' Angela Aneke said, 'and that's why you have to start early. When you're financing your property, you're doing it with future flows.'

Even banks usually want to know about your income stream and how many more years you'll be in employment. So if you're in your late twenties or early thirties, start now.

Another wise counsel is, 'If you were supposed to plant a tree twenty-five years ago and you didn't, the next best time to plant it is now.'

Don't wait until you have all the money before considering real estate investment. The starting point is to consider, research, and understand the real estate opportunities that exist. You don't need money in your pocket to consider a field. Be bold enough to consider it. Make sure you're not wasting time and Passing Over Opportunities Repeatedly: becoming P.O.O.R.

Start investing for your children as soon as you can; if you can afford it, start when they are in university. As I said earlier, make them landlords instead of tenants while they are at school, especially in an area where accommodation is scarce. Their friends and fellow students can become their first tenants.

Is there a right time to invest in real estate? It's always a good time to invest if you are armed with these three things:

- a clear vision and goal
- the right information from the right team
- the right strategy

Don't wait to buy real estate. Buy real estate and then wait.

X

X-RAY LENS

'When you pay attention to detail, the big picture will take care of itself.' – Georges St-Pierre

X is for X-Ray Lens. Before you say yes to the deal, get an X-ray. This could be a trusted professional advisor or a personal background check or both. Do not be in such in a hurry that you skip your due diligence.

Y

YOU

'Don't apologise for expressing passion. Don't back down when it comes to your integrity. Don't let anyone undermine your standards for the sake of ease. Be a character of excellence, not excuses.' – Janna Cachola

Y is for You. You are the most important success factor. Your preferences and experiences could be valuable. There are six main real estate categories:

- residential
- commercial
- retail
- industrial
- hospitality
- mixed use

Which do you prefer? You are unlikely to be successful investing in something you feel no connection to, just because it makes money. Ibukun Awosika once explained, 'Do you know where I have major interest in property development? Low-cost housing. I want to build single-room apartments to provide accommodation. There is a social angle to it.'

Be true to yourself.

For instance, if you're a spiritual person, you shouldn't leave that side of yourself out of your real estate investing.

For Angela Aneke, the favour of God is the number one success factor in real estate investing. 'I don't believe you can buy property without the favour of God,' she said. She saw the hand of God in her first investment, which was in Ghana. She wanted to rent a place, and the landlord said, 'You want to rent? Why not buy?'

'All I have is my one year's rent,' she said. So he lent her the down payment, which was 40 per cent. The landlord actually lent it to her; wow.

When she went to take a loan for the balance, the Ghana Home Loans chairman turned out to be an old colleague.

'If you've been faithful in building God's house, he will help you build yours,' she said.

Subu Giwa-Amu also draws strength and confidence from her faith when investing. 'Once you step into a project bigger than you,' she said, 'God will back you up. Start sowing into building God's house, and He will show up for you.'

Bring some of your personality to the investment, where reasonable. This is not always applicable, but in small-scale investments, it could be a real edge.

Z

Z?

> 'It is a comfortable feeling to know that you stand on your own ground. Land is about the only thing that can't fly away.' – Anthony Trollope

Z is for Z? The Z factor is the unknown in real estate. Real estate is probably one of the safest asset classes, stable and not subject to dramatic fluctuations. However, as with anything in life, nothing is without risks. Everything in life has risks; you can't run away from them.

You can manage and mitigate most risks that arise, but there are some things in life, and real estate, that you can't plan for. If you want a 100 per cent safe life, then do absolutely nothing, and even that doesn't guarantee you safety. Follow this book's approach from A to Y, and don't worry about things you cannot change.

These are some major issues affecting real estate investors:

- access to finance
    - Mortgage finance in Nigeria is still in its infancy; we have inadequate credit facilities for investors; where available, the interest rates are very high.

- - An imperfect mortgage system due to the absence of a strong secondary mortgage market, lack of uniform mortgage underwriting standards, and few conforming mortgage assets.
- Policy and regulation
  - The Land Use Act (1978) continues to dictate and hinder the land market in Nigeria. To date, the objectives of the act have not been achieved, and further to this, the law has led to further distortion and abuse of citizens' rights to access and own land.
- the lack of easy access to land and high cost of land for building
- the lack of effective intergovernmental collaboration (e.g., federal, state, and local government) for investors building projects
- the prevalence of slums in all urban centres that require upgrading
- the absence of a mechanism for mobilising and channelling construction finance
- the absence of a National Collateral Registry
- the long period it takes to obtain development permit and to access funds for buildings.

Despite these challenges, many people, including women, are building. This tells you that there are really no excuses to hold you back. There's room for everybody in real estate, whatever your personal goals are.

By investing in real estate, you can have a good life, impact others, and contribute to building the future of an emerging economy. Real estate investment gives you the opportunity to live a life of purpose, a life of passion, and it opens you up to possibilities.

'I haven't made a better investment than real estate,' Angela Aneke said.

Neither have I. I hope you don't allow your fears to stop you from securing your financial future.

ABOUT THE AUTHOR

UDO MARYANNE OKONJO is currently the chief executive officer and vice chair of Fine and Country West Africa, where she leads the management and team of champions in building the future of Nigeria's Real Estate. Under her leadership, Fine and Country has captured a niche in the Nigeria real estate sector, providing specialised advisory, corporate leasing, marketing, and sales of luxury residential and commercial projects to leading real estate developers, high net worth investors and institutional clients.

Udo was admitted to both the Nigerian and New York Bars in 1991 and 1994 respectively, and

pursued a successful legal career, rising to become a partner in a leading Nigerian law firm. She was also a Senior Special Adviser on Legal and Constitutional Matters to the President of the Senate of Nigeria.

Udo was best graduating female student in 1991 at the Nigerian Law School, and was awarded the prestigious Chevening Scholarship to study at the University of London, Kings College School of Law, where she graduated with a master's degree in Law (LLM), specialising in Corporate and Commercial Law. She is also an alumnus of the Executive Business Programs at the Said Business School, Oxford University High Performance Leadership Programme, and the Cambridge Judge Business School, Cambridge University, where she took part in the executive programmes earning a certificate over the course of her two years study. Udo also participates in the Oxford Real Estate Society.

She is very passionate about leadership development in all sectors of the economy and was instrumental in setting up Nigeria's premier Real Estate Leaders Network and the Institute of Real Estate Excellence, amongst other learning platforms including the Lagos Business School and Fine and Country led Real Estate Leadership Development Executive Programme for Professionals and Investors. An astute real estate investor and trusted advisor, Udo is passionate about real estate as a means of wealth creation and nation building. Working with Fine and Country, she set up the Finer Wealth Club, the first women's group to enable more women to get onto the property ladder as a means of securing their financial future and empowering them to make better life choices. This book is an effort to encourage women to gain clarity, confidence, and competence in this very important area.

Visit her online on www.udookonjo.com and the Finer Wealth Club on www.thefinerwealthclub.com

www.ingramcontent.com/pod-product-compliance
Lightning Source LLC
Chambersburg PA
CBHW030816180526
45163CB00003B/1304